OLD TIMES IN HORRY COUNTY

Published by The History Press
Charleston, SC 29403
www.historypress.net

Copyright © 2007 by Randall A. Wells
All rights reserved

Cover image: Andrew Stanley. *By Bob Graham*.

All drawings courtesy of artist Bob Graham.

First published 2007

Manufactured in the United Kingdom

ISBN 978.1.59629.189.8

Library of Congress Cataloging-in-Publication Data

Wells, Randall A., 1942-
  Old times in Horry County : a narrative history / Randall A. Wells.
     p. cm.
  Includes bibliographical references.
  ISBN-13: 978-1-59629-189-8 (alk. paper)
  1. Horry County (S.C.)--History--Anecdotes. 2. Horry County (S.C.)--Social life and
customs--Anecdotes. 3. Horry County (S.C.)--Biography--Anecdotes. 4. Oral history.
I. Title.
  F277.H6W45 2007
  975.7'8704--dc22
                              2007018298

OLD TIMES IN HORRY COUNTY

A NARRATIVE HISTORY

Randall A. Wells

RANDALL A. WELLS

WITH AN INTRODUCTION BY DR. CHARLES JOYNER

Charleston • London

The
History
PRESS

Contents

To the late Catherine Heniford Lewis.

Foreword

The Horry County of my boyhood is fading into memory. Many of the old landmarks are gone now, and the landscape is being changed beyond recognition. It is a temptation for those of us who have lived here a long time to spend more time lamenting what we have lost than rejoicing in what we have gained. Many of the changes are good, and some of them wonderful. All parts of the county benefit from the outstanding new medical facilities in Conway, Loris, Myrtle Beach, North Myrtle Beach and Surfside Beach. The county's extraordinary population growth has brought newcomers who have made outstanding contributions to their new home. The growth of Coastal Carolina University and Horry-Georgetown Technical College has been of great help to a county that lacked local opportunities for higher education until the 1950s.

Still, the county I grew up in seemed destined to live only in the memories of the old. When the old died, the memories would be lost. At least that is the way it seemed in 1990, when Randall Wells, a professor of English and speech at Coastal Carolina University, came to me with a proposal for a history of Horry County not learned from books, but from the people who had made it. He had recently interviewed some of the county's elders with a camcorder in the course of writing his book, *Along the Waccamaw: A Yankee Discovers a Home by the River.* He asked if the Waccamaw Center for Historical and Cultural Studies, which I directed, could provide some modest financial support for purchasing videotapes and having the interviews transcribed. I was impressed with the infectious energy and enthusiasm of this scholar who was no longer willing to confine his scholarship to books alone. *Along the Waccamaw* had already revealed his deep affection for Horry County and its people. And I recognized the enduring importance of the project he proposed. I told him the center would sponsor his project enthusiastically if his interviews could be recorded on broadcast-quality tapes by Coastal Carolina's Media Center. That brought David Parker and W. Press Courtney into the project. I had worked with them before, and I knew they were more than just camera and sound technicians. They are consummate artists whose contribution to the project has been crucial.

Soon Randall Wells was joined by his remarkable friend and colleague, Catherine Heniford Lewis, a retired librarian who had assembled an important local history collection in the county library and seemed to know everybody in the county. He describes her as "the main contact and interviewer of the project for several years" before her death in 1998, while he describes himself as "her apprentice." But over the next seventeen years, the apprentice became the master, crisscrossing Horry County to conduct interviews with Horry County's elders. They were men and women, black and white, the living libraries of Horry history, their experiences surviving in the act of their telling it. Randall became their friend and they became his teachers.

As a result of his extraordinary odyssey, the Horry County Oral History Project grew to an extraordinary collection of more than one hundred interviews, most of them housed in the Kimbel Library at Coastal Carolina University, carefully transcribed into typescripts and catalogued with appropriate finding aids for each interview. The finding aids make them useful for students and scholars alike. The majority of the original tapes are also preserved in a climate-controlled environment, offering an invaluable resource to linguistic scholars and others.

The project enabled the Waccamaw Center to produce a series of television documentaries on Horry County history. I was the producer of *Voices of History*, which featured Randall Wells and Catherine Heniford Lewis introducing excerpts from their interviews. Wells subsequently produced three more documentaries from the interviews, *Horry Stories*, *Wood & Water* and *No Match for Our Dad*. All three were directed by David Parker and W. Press Courtney, and one was shown on South Carolina public television.

The oral histories were at the heart of Randall's 2004 book, *Swamp, Strand, and Steamboat: Voices of Horry County, South Carolina, 1732-1954*. Organized thematically, each chapter draws from a wide range of interviews, as well as from documents in the Horry County Historical Society's *Independent Republic Quarterly* and other published sources.

The present book, *Old Times in Horry County: A Narrative History*, includes transcripts of interviews with thirteen of the county's living libraries as well as Wells' own eloquent meditations on the county and its history. In it he compiles testimonies not only from his own interviews, but also from the pioneering interviews of Burgin Berry, Carl E. Compton, Etrulia P. Dozier, Billy Holliday and Catherine Lewis. These interviews reveal thirteen individuals, dredging up the hopes and dreams of a lifetime from the depths of their memories to the surface of their consciousness, telling of memorable events and daily life in the authentic voice of the people. Consider, for example, Rilla McCrackin's poetic description of her childhood as a sharecropper's daughter:

When I was eleven,
electricity finally come through to our house.
We had only lights, no running water.
Still no bathroom.
We had to pump the water.

Every few years
we would move to another location.
The winters didn't get any warmer
and the summers didn't get any cooler.

I was eighteen
before we got a bathroom,
and it was not in the house.

The water would freeze
in the commode at night.
It was in a hulled up room
on the back porch.

We never had a hot water heater
until I was married
with children.
Three children anyway.

The oral memoirs in this book evoke both joy and melancholy. Drawn from varied lifetimes, they tie together the varied strands of Horry County's society and culture. They are significant not only for the history they tell, but also for the lyrical language of their telling. These testimonies preserve at least some of Horry County's fading memories for posterity.

Most of these Horry stories follow a similar pattern. They tell of hard times back then, especially during the Great Depression, when people had to strive to survive and toil to make things easier for their children. And they *did* toil and strive. And they *did* survive and make things easier for their children. They are proud of much that was gained by their effort, but they miss much that was lost. Thinking back, some of the older ones remember those days as some of the happiest times of their lives.

Permeating all of these testimonies are stories of change and continuity, sometimes in fits and starts, sometimes one right after the other, sometimes both at the same time. They tell of creating a better quality of life for the generations to follow, but they also tell of a way of life that has been lost. Nostalgia for the past is one way of dealing with a scary present. But those of us who see growth and development as threats might well gain perspective on our growing pains by comparing our county to its neighbors that are *losing* population. Both growth and development are inevitable, but neither is inevitably good or inevitably bad. Horry County has seen both kinds in the past century, and the present one offers the prospect of both kinds in the future.

The stories in this book suggest important benchmarks, not only for the world we have lost, but also for the world we have gained. Understanding the way we were is essential to understanding what we have become and what we are becoming.

Charles W. Joyner

Acknowledgements

For many kinds of help, many people are acknowledged in individual chapters.

For its articles and indexes (the latter compiled by Catherine Heniford Lewis), the *Independent Republic Quarterly* (*IRQ*), published by the Horry County Historical Society, 1967–present.

For her precedent and her advice, Pamela Grundy, author of *You Always Think of Home: A Portrait of Clay County, Alabama* (Athens: Univ. of Georgia Press, 1991).

For recommending the pencil of Bob Graham, Sudie Payne Daves. For providing a photographic basis for his art, Bill Edmonds, who long ago took classic shots of Andrew Stanley and Flossie Morris; Dennis Reed, who converted videotape frames to still shots; Paul Olsen, whose shutter opened to axe and chimney; and relatives and friends of the interviewees, especially the Carr family and Nellie Holmes Johnson.

For their ace transcriptions, Ann M. Ipock and the late Ann Glesenkamp. And for their videography and equally good company, David Parker and W. Press Courtney.

ACKNOWLEDGEMENTS

For supplying a liberal amount of postage and photocopying, the Thomas W. and Robin W. Edwards College of Humanities and Fine Arts, Coastal Carolina University.

For their expertise, professors Eldred E. Prince, Stephen J. Nagle, Veronica Gerald and Sallie Clarkson of Coastal Carolina University, as well as Dr. J. William F. ("Billy") Holliday.

For recommending improvements in wording, Andrea Wells Vasaune.

For inviting me to write the book and for working with me on it, Jenny Kaemmerlen, Commissioning Editor, The History Press. For her sharp eye and amiable manner, Christine Langill, Project Editor, The History Press.

For her support and patience through yet another final book, Marjory B. Wells.

Introduction

The six-year-old boy woke up before day and walked to school through the winter cold. He had to cross several creeks on foot-logs, for although Wannamaker Community was at the tip of the county, it was still in the Lowcountry, where water is a given, like gravity. Gary crossed at the Grantham farm and circled around where Rafe Grainger's—do you know John D. Hook's place?—came back in just this side of the church, then followed it down and cut across down there at the other side of the Jim Anderson farm. At school he was glad to see his classmate, Douglas.

Seventy-six years later, the longtime friends met again and enjoyed being interviewed by their mutual friend, Catherine Heniford Lewis of the Horry County Oral History Project. Seventeen years after that, the two classmates come together again in *Old Times in Horry County: A Narrative History*—along with other citizens whose portraits are drawn in both graphite and words.

When these two pals, born in 1907, started first grade, the oldest of the people in this book was already thirty-two; as a child she had accompanied her mother on steamboat excursions. Another, a child of a Civil War veteran, had just started her long career as a schoolteacher, while another was a boy whose schooling would be measured only in days. Another was already a timberman whom Uncle Sam would soon pull out of the woods like a log on a cable and then ship abroad. Another was a logger and a ferryman, while another lived near the Little Pee Dee River in a community named for a defunct ferry. Several interviewees were not yet born, and the youngest was born in the fifty-seventh year of the oldest.

This book compiles interviews with thirteen people—male and female, black and white, town and country, schooled and unschooled. Two chapters record joint interviews, while several other chapters record multiple interviews with the same person. These interviews have been chosen from among either the hundred or so sponsored by the Horry County Oral History Project or the thirty or so salvaged by the project as audiotapes, videotapes or transcripts of earlier interviews.

In 1989, the author switched from videotaping his students in his public speaking class to videotaping people he described in *Along the Waccamaw: A Yankee Discovers a Home by the River* (Algonquin 1990). Abetted by the camera, lights and cables of David Parker and W. Press Courtney of the college's Media Center, the venture seemed promising, so Wells asked Charles W. Joyner, Burroughs Professor of History, if the Waccamaw Center could somehow formalize it. Immediately it became christened and sponsored, with Wells promoted to director.

Wells soon asked Catherine Heniford Lewis, chief librarian of the county, to interview her friend, Miss Evelyn Snider, at her house overlooking Kingston Lake in Conway. That experiment successful, Catherine became the main contact and interviewer for several years, while the director became her apprentice. The Project thrived because of her familiarity with the area (equaled by her affection for it), her range of acquaintances, her perceptiveness, her diplomacy and her longtime work with the historical society. Catherine herself would write *Horry County, South Carolina, 1770-1993* (Columbia: Univ. of South Carolina Press, 1998).

Over the years, the Horry County Oral History Project arranged, conducted and transcribed interviews and it gave a home to others already recorded or transcribed. It also secured release forms for all interviews and tapes, most of which were deposited in Kimbel Library on campus. The project ran from 1989 through 2006. To measure this span in the event-fashion of human memory, during the first interview, the nine-year-old daughter of the author romped with dogs near the Waccamaw River, and soon after the last interview, she walked with him down the aisle of a church.

This book captures some of the drama of oral historiography. For one thing, it records the surprisingly diverse origins of these interviews. For another, it reveals behind-the-scene challenges, technical or otherwise. Moreover, it describes the interviewee's surroundings and appearance and suggests his or her particular variety of language. In fact, the author reviewed all but one transcription against the videotape or audiotape. He has sometimes corrected the transcription (i.e., from "whole layer of seeds" to "Crotalaria seeds"), has always made it closer (more precise as to grammar and pronunciation) and has recorded nonverbal details. These include facial expressions, gestures that emphasize or describe, and paralanguage, a term for vocal sounds that accompany words, such as laughter, timbre of the voice, pace, volume or even silence. These nonverbal signals interact with each other and with the words themselves in a rich, communicative mixture.

The original question-and-answer dialogue has been transformed into a monologue to gain space and focus. The author has chosen excerpts from the interviews but has kept them in the original sequence, however unpredictable or even disjointed, however many lines or pages apart in the transcription. The passages may be edited for readability, but never for meaning. For example:

Transcription:

Interviewee: They was a lot of fun people…I think back and that used to be a lively place…the ones that lived there, they really didn't think they could live anywheres else.
Interviewer: Why didn't they?
Interviewee: Well, it was home to 'em.

Book:

They was a lot of fun people. Lord a mercy, I think back and that Ferry used to be a lively place—they really didn't think they could ever live anywheres else. It was home to 'em.

The second version omits not only the interviewer's question, but also the ellipses and the redundancy ("the ones that lived there"). It also includes an exclamation from the audiotape ("Lord a mercy") and adds one word for clarity ("Ferry" for "there").

These chapters proceed clockwise, though not chronologically, around South Carolina's largest county, pronounced "Oh-Ree."

The first chapter begins at the far southeast (five or six o'clock) with David Carr, centenarian and World War I veteran, who remembers Myrtle Beach, Surfside Beach, Socastee and Burgess. The second chapter crosses to the west of the Waccamaw River and Bucksville, home of the redoubtable "Flossie" Morris. The next chapter moves up the river to Conway for an interview conducted in 1970 with two elderly half-sisters,

Lillie B. Latimer and Ruth C. "Sabe" Woodbury, whose mother ran the concession on the riverboat. The next chapter moves farther up the Waccamaw for an interview that ends at the riverside itself with Link Vereen, once a ferryman. The next chapter returns downriver and up Kingston Lake Swamp to Crabtree Swamp, near the home of Woodrow W. Long—veteran, mailman, farmer. The next chapter moves to the northwest for Carrie D. Doyle's memoir of the Galivants Ferry community, while the one after that stays in that general area, but presents the vivid recollections of a sharecropper's daughter, Rilla C. McCrackin. The next chapter moves to twelve o'clock and Wannamaker, home of Gary M. Mincey, an early game warden, and of Douglas B. Bailey, who was able to go from picking cotton to dispensing medicine. The next dips to the southeast and the town of Loris, home of S.F. Horton, an early figure in agricultural improvement. The next chapter flies like a bird down Simpson Creek to the Waccamaw, and then crosses the inseparable river and swamp to the farm of Andrew Stanley, who used to build rafts of logs and "mind 'em" off the bank toward Conway Lumber Company. The last chapter returns to the coast at Myrtle Beach, before the Strand was Grand, and to the memories of an early restaurateur, Julia P. Macklen.

Randall A. Wells

David Carr.

David Carr

Born 1887

"Put me down, I ain't no baby."

As a boy, Carl E. Compton (1921-2006) liked to hear one of his grandfather's friends, Mr. Billy, talk about the old days. In 1987, as the new pastor emeritus of the First Baptist Church in Myrtle Beach—where he had served since 1949—he made a decision with the encouragement of others. He would interview citizens of Horry County in order to preserve "things that are not written in any history books but would be interesting for us to share" (D. Carr transcript, p. 1). Thus was born *Hearing Horry History*. Compton ("Dr. C") held the sessions mainly on the wood-paneled set of Channel 43, WGSE, Myrtle Beach (owned by Dove Broadcasting); the sessions were filmed by Dennis Reed. Compton deposited the master copies of the three-quarter-inch videotapes, no fewer than thirty-seven of them, in Chapin Memorial Library.[1]

Dr. C's very first interview was with David Carr, a child of slaves, who had recently turned one hundred years old. On the videotape, David sits with a black fedora hanging from the corner of his rocking chair. His skin is quite dark, his face deeply creased, his bearing serious and self-possessed. His original teeth seem to be intact, and he often works the corner of his mouth. He wears a dark gray suit with a white handkerchief in the pocket, and his white tie, striped with blue and reddish brown, has a loosely tied double Windsor knot. The interview, one of Compton's many contributions to Myrtle Beach, is an invaluable record of personality, folk life and events—especially a black soldier's experience in World War I, when he unexpectedly applied his logging skills to a military campaign.

The interview records language, too—not only Dave's unique way of speaking, but his African-influenced variety of English. In 1995, the transcriber, Ann M. Ipock, was challenged by his pronunciation, vocabulary and grammar, all echoes of Gullah culture along the coast of South Carolina. Based on her work, refinements were made by the author; by Esther Rebecca Holmes (Mr. Carr's daughter); by her daughter, Mrs. Doris Turman; and by Caroline Burgess and Earlene York (Dave's other granddaughters). Then the author made an even closer transcription. Finally, Professor Veronica Gerald, who knew Dave, applied her ear to the tape and made further changes, most notably correcting the lyrics of the first song.

Well, the section I lived in, was born at, the place was called the Old Ark [a plantation]. But now it's named Surfside and my fo'eparents were slave.[2] When I come along, we de colored didn't have no school. And the way I learned to read, a man had a store called Old Man John Vereen. He had a boy, me and him were the same year, named Bossy. He'd go to school and he'd come back in de evening, play with me, say, "David, you ought to be able to read and write your name." I say, "I don't know how." We didn't had no books, so we'd get on the ground and sign off and tek a stick or your finger and write your name. First thing he done, he had a old school book called *Baby Ray*.[3] And he gave me that book and he'd learn me my ABCs.

"Shine! What that is?" "Them ABCs." Say, "Well, that's the starting o' your letter." And he'd write it and I'd spell it; and I got to spellin' it he say, "Now you got to spell it by heart. You *can* do it." I say, "Who? Me?" I say, "A, B, C, D, E, F, G...[goes all the way to Q]." He say, "You musta been to school some." I say, "I been up to school there in the Gawd." [Points skyward.] Went on for about five years. I learned more 'n he did and could tell him he lesson. Yes. A gift from a friend. And Gawd.

My parents farm and pick cotton and hoe corn and plow and ditch. We didn't had no tractor, nothing then—few people, big shot, had mule and buggy. There was no buggy or road cya't [cart]. After awhile the buggy come out and most of the colored people then and a few white didn't had anything but a ox and a cart. And the crippled people or couldn't walk, they have a big goat mek a little wagon and git in there and drive or ride, go where they want.

Some of it is [the same crops as today], but we used to raise cotton and corn, peanut and peas and potato, they called it white potato. We didn't had no yalla' 'tata [sweet potato] then. Great Gawd, man, we had rice gone to bed. Yes, and meat. [Illustrates each stage with his hands.] And we'd go in the woods and saw a tree down and take ya a' ahxe and hatchet and chop around it and put some clay around the edge of it and buil' a fire and then keep chinking it until it get it and mek a mortar out of it. Then we go mek a pestle, cut a pestle and peel it in the middle, left two end and sharpen it down and we go in the mortar and beat rice. [Illustrates process with hands.] Fine.

Then we'd shell corn and we had no mill but we had a hand mill, you mighta read about that [illustrates with hands]. You put it up and put the stopper in it and put a stick on it and you turn it and it turn the thing and you put your corn in deah and if you want fine corn, you drop it down. If you want thick, big corn you raised up a little bit. Yes, sir. Go to store to buy the sugar.

Yes, I grew up in the Burgess area [between Socastee and Georgetown County along the present Highway 707]. At Socastee they had about three sto'es there—four stores. They had Cooper, Clardy and this other man I told you about we got their house there, and then another old man 'cross the bridge had a store. That's all the store we had. And when we come down to Buhgiss [ponders]—Old Man Johnny Vereen had a store and Isaac Patrick had a store and Old Man Marlowe had a store. They stocked all but light bread [wheat bread rather than cornbread]. If you get light bread or ice we had to go to Georgetown and carry sawdust in a sack and buy a piece o' ice and put it in the sack and tie it up and put it in the shade and when we got home, dig a hole under the house and put the sack and the ice down and kiver it up. Fifty pounds of ice. You go by ox and kyart [cart]. Oh, we'd go deah in a dee [day]. We didn't spend [chuckles] no motel or stay with anybody, some of them people house; stay in the place with the train and the boats would land—the deck. They had a room there that you buy your ticket to go on the train and we could sleep in there. [Shakes head.] No train didn't run no farrer than Conway and Georgetown. And later it built a road from Eenah [Aynor, a village northeast of Conway] right on through Conway and stay dere a while and then they built it to come to Myrtle Beach.[4]

I used to walk deah many time to Conway many a time and ride the train right down Main Street. And after a while the train by mekin' smoke, the people got to claiming that it damaged the furniture and the stuff in the stores and they move it on the outside of Conway [in 1928].

[Re: the upcoming celebration of the third millennium.] Well, we didn't had nothing like this. When the old year go out and the new year come in we had Watch Night. And someone would watch and when the mornin' star rise, hear 'm say, "The mornin' star rise" and when he go to the west [points finger and sweeps arm to his left], he look to see the mornin' star come up. And then just before daylight, the old people got to singin' [sings]:

Loss Mossa bahn key
Send them chillun de hunt 'um.
Haunt 'em, chillun hunt 'um
Hunt 'um till you fin' 'um.

[Dave smiles.] And another old man after awhile he'd get up and sing:

Day, day, day, day'd a-comin'
Jumping in Deruclum [Jerusalem]
Hallelujah, hallelujah

You see [slavery owned our foreparents] two hundred and twenty years. Selling as common hog. And when us come free—the fourth of March—we didn't had no home. [Pauses.] And no school. [Pauses.] And no church. [Pauses.] And they didn't had no *po*lice then but they had something they called *pat*rol. They'd catch ya and—didn't had no jailhouse—and Mossa have a driver to beat you. And when they have the sale, the man come they buying the people and the people 'round there crying. [Twiddles his thumbs.]

And man had [two] parrot and he know, them parrot, knowed all the colored people. And them people being in the field working, stop and lean up on the hoe and that parrot would know either one of them by name. Say, "Old Mossa [spoken in a confidential tone], that damn nigger is out there leaning up on the hoe." "Who is, Dave?" "Oh, so-and-so." [Chuckles.] Yeah, and he'd tell de mossa. The mossa come say, "Well, one gone over the fence." Mossa say maybe he gone out there to do his business. "It don't take a damn nigger that long to do his business." [Laughs and claps hands.] And Mossa—he'd sit on that chair and hab his driver to gie the woman twenty-five licks [flicks arm downward] and the man fifty.

[Compton, a navy chaplain in the Second World War, asks if the first war had affected Carr.] I went to World War I. I register in Conway. They tell you really nothin' about no war then. "Now you want to tell your occupation, whatever you can do and do do—tell it and we'll write it." Me—I've went foreman in nineteen-nine—engineer, barber and a cook and a railroad mahstuh [master]. They gave me a 'ploma for it.[5]

Whenever I was working to Dunn, North C'lina, in the logwood and come to the post—had a old wood bok [box] there for da put your mail in—and I went to the mailbox and I see a letter in there for me and I take it out. Uncle Sahm, he got his finger on the letter like that [points at Dr. Compton], say "I want you." I say "Good God almighty." Next morning I worked with a bunch of men down in [place name unclear] came through. I went down there, said, "Boys, I won't be here too long now. I got to go to service." "Why?" "Well, I got a letter from president and he say he want me and I got to go." I say, "But you know what I done?" Say, "No." "I cussed that man out." "Well, Captain Dave, ain't you know if you cuss a president, they'll kill you." I say, "Yeah, but he didn't hear me, he was in the White House and I's down inside the swamp. [Laughter.] So he don't know what I say."

And I come home and my wife [Maude] and my mother and my brothers and sisters and uncle. "Why you come home for, Dave?" Say, "I just come home to see ya'll. I'm gonna make a move from where we was settin' there an' gwine to Aynor. Thought I'd let ya'll know." And I walked to Conway that day and gwine to the courthouse and I hear my name called.

The next morning load us on the train and carry us to Camp Jackson [in Columbia]. And they met upstairs. I could look on, from the hospital, look on Camp Jackson. And I stay there three days and they send me to Newport News, Virginia. I stayed there about two week. Then they tell us, "Now, you want to get your clothes pack up and we going to catch the boat and gwine cross that river"—didn't tell us we were gwine oversea. And we load up on that ship and five hundred head of men. And they get us a—what do you call—[folds arms around his chest] so if you fall overboard... Yeah, life jacket.

So, we got on there and when I realize we was on the sea [lifts arm and points to his left], we was coming long—right along the ocean—you see when you gwine over there they set you compass wi' da sunrise. And when you come back [points with right arm], they set it with the sun down you come south. Every morning you set it and the sun rise when

Soldier Carr.

you gwine. And they'd carry it right on over to France. In the evening, when you set it, it would bring you right on back. And when I got off— see a lot of the mans white and black didn't been on the sea and they get seasick. But see, I raise right there by the ocean—to the Ark. So people get seasick and they puke on there and dirty on the ship and when they tek 'em off, they load off to France. He say, "David, now you take these men and clean this ship up. And we come back down this evening and get you—and he gone." So we clean it up and when I come out, I look up on the boat [stares upward] and the thing had registered 3,556 mile o' water. Say, "Good God." And after we got out there about five days, they tell us, fifteen days and night to go over because we have to watch for these sub-planes bombing in the water [i.e., mines]. Didn't take us but ten days to come back [after the war].

When I got off the ship and gwine up on there, I meet a old French and he had a wooden shoe with hay sticking in for a stocking [holds up fingers of one hand]. He say, "Majoo, mashay." I say, "I come all the way over here and you come here cussin' me." Another man understan' him say, "No, Sergeant, he say you, 'Good morning.'" [Laughter.] I said, "Well, I tell him, you tell him 'Comment-allez vous.'" I meet a woman with a baby in her hand [crosses arms to illustrate]—I used to love chillin—and I say, "Mrs., you got a pretty baby," she shake up her shoulder and say, "No compris." [More anecdotes follow.]

After the armistice sign [on November 11, 1918, when David was 31], we gone up there fightin' morely. Sail from Newport News to Brest, France, and from Brest, France, to no man land. Where nobody don't live. And I was out there as a railroad master; dey'd blow up the railroad. [He illustrates the following process with winding and cutting hand gestures.] And I'd take rail on the train ties and a saw and a drill so they could cut the rail and could bore a hole through it, put bolts in it and cool it down. One evenin' we was down there and blow up a road and I had done fixed it back and trains [were] out there. Man looking out the window at me like that [he peers to the left and downward over his left arm, which rests on the windowsill of the locomotive-rocking chair]. When I got it done I love it. "Whoop-whoop-woo!" [makes a "come-ahead" wave] he run on in, and after he get on in, "Whoop-woo!" [smiles as he waves "Come-on-back"], she back out.

I wrote and ask myself, God, send me to France to tear up the road, had nothing to tote [with] over there. Had to pull the guns with mule and horse. And when some of the men didn't even know how to put a bridle on the mule. And they bog down, they'd come get me and all rushin' back.

Fifteen and twenty minutes after I get there I'd have a gun on the hill [lifts arm toward point in distance]. Horse and all. They pick me up, tote me there. I'd say [spoken dryly], "Put me down, I ain't no baby."[6]

Den I was mustard gas' three time. And you don't live [through] that mustard gas. Nothin' affect but me eye.[7]

Yes sir, came back to Burgess in 1919.[8] [Removes glasses and rubs left eye with hand before explaining how slaves came to own land.] Well, the younger one—the one doin' the proper buyin'—them slave people live on the Mossa place after the war [Civil War], and if they fail to go on and farm and he tell them, you tell them you either got to go now or move and they had nowhere to move. So they had to go. No school, no church, nothing. And after we come 'long…my mother hoe corn and cotton and tobacco and peanuts 'n rice for thirty cent a day, ten hours, and I was a knee-pants boy and they give me fifteen cent a day. We had a better time then, than we did now. I had no pocketbook. I'd take my money and go by a pine tree and dig in the dirt down there and put (you know) a snuff box, or somethin' and kiver it and put straw in it.

The first piece of lan' I bought, it was five acres and I had to give a dollar and a quarter a acre. Then some more people buy some and didn't pay the tak [tax] and mortgage and the tax took it. Some of them dead and didn't had the money to bury them and didn't, but they had no bought coffin then, you had to, mind, take a old thing and bohd [board] and square it down [pushes hand outward] and make a casket. And put you in it.

[Someone else's unpaid loan and taxes helped him buy property.] One fellow had one hundred and ten acres and he ga' the man a mortgage on the lahn [land] to bury Daddy; and I don't know how much it cost to bury him, I wasn't 'eah. And didn't pay no tax on the place. I was fishing on the beach and the [debtor] come and told me, "You know what I do?" I say, "Whaddat?" "I wanta borrow three hundred dollars from you." [Pauses.] I say, "I don't have three hundred on me. I got three hundred but it in the bank." "Well give it to me and [here's] the deed for the place till I pay you back." I go on there and take him to Conway and ga' him the three hundred and 'fore he pay me back, he catch his wife selling liquor—old stumphole liquor—and they put him in jail. [Chuckles, removes his glasses to rub his left eye again.] And he was a switchman porter on the train from Conway, and so he lost his job. He didn't pay nothin', and didn't let me know nothin' and I didn't know anything till the land was up for sale. White man called Lee Outlaw [unintelligible]. "Dave, didn't they say he had mortgage that place to you for three hundred?" "Yeah." Say, "Well, it's up for sale now. You go and pay up the man three hundred and pay up the tax, you'll have that place." So I went and pay 'em the three hundred and run up the tax, and the tax had behind six years. And I pay that up. About two hundred. It was one hundred and ten acres of lan' and two building was on it."

Yes sir. We walk heah [to Myrtle Beach]. Wasn't nothing but one store there and a boardwalk for walking and no street, just a boardwalk—the street was so sandy. That's right, they called [the company store] Chapin. And when they cleaned up them farm—them big farm on Myrtle Beach there—Conway Lumber Company come over here and bought the timber. I snaked [pulled them to a central place with a draft animal] the log and they pay me extra to pull the tops, kind of up together [joins hands together at fingertips], so they could burn it. That whole farm, I did.[9]

Yes, they [summer visitors] come on the boat down the Waccamaw River. They'd come to Conway on the train and then they get daylight and catch the boat and come on down to Peachtree Landin' or, well, different landin'. [They would go into Myrtle Beach] on foot. Or they'd hire somebody with the ox 'n cart, mule 'n wagon. They'd take them down to the beach. And the women dressed then with long [unintelligible] pants and then when they'd see us coming, they'd pull that down [roll down their trouser legs]. Now it's up here and they'd see us coming and pull it up. [Laughs.]

[Dr. Compton asks him to re-tell his experience of becoming a Christian.] Well, I thought I was raised up by a religion-hearted grandmother. She was a Indian but she was a doctor. And my great grand-granddaddy was a black Jew, and my daddy was a N-e-g-r-o, so I got three-blooded dog in me. I'll bite you if you mess with me. [Looks sideways with menacing expression as Compton laughs.] And my grandmother would teach me the Bible and the way to live. She told me—I never forgot it—say, "Son, the Bible say 'Honor thy mother and father and your days shall be long upon the land which is the Lord thy God giveth' and 'Do unto others as you would have them do unto they own self.'" [Reveals that he had no intention of following the latter injunction but eventually changed his mind.]

I know a boy come down the beach where I was fishing at—a white boy—and drinking and messin' with women down there and loss his pocketbook with one hundred and fifty dollars in it. Come back next morning, couldn't find his pocketbook, crying. I had it. I say, "What did you loss?" [Dave hints at a whimper:] "I lost my pocketbook." "How much money was in it?" He told me. "What's your name?" He told me. I say "Here—this it?" [Presents imaginary wallet.] And he was so glad he was going to give me ten dollars. I said, "No. You go ahead, and be particular and not loss what you got." And a white boy come down 'ere on the beach. He come from overseas, said. He didn't had no money and nowhere to stay and I let him stay in the fishing camp and feed him and let him fish with me and make a little money till he got ready to get enough money to go somewhere else.

Well, I had many [good memories]. But the [most] blessed I had that I get out the day when I go oversea and four head of men get shot right 'side—and I could see him *gapping* and the blood [spurting] out and I looked down on 'em and I say, "Lord, you got all the power in your hands. If you'll save me, I'll serve you the balance of my days." And a white man come up with a pencil and a paper [looks down at imaginary paper in his hand] 'n call me by my name. Said, "David." I said, "Yes, sir." "I'll write your name but you wouldn't have a friend in the world," I'd say "Right." "I'd write your name but the world will talk about you," I'd say "Right." "I'd write your name but your name would be stick upon every milepost when you write it and you know what that represent?" I said, "No, sir." "That would represent the Father, the Son and the Holy Ghost." And he walked away.

And that Lord got to picking up off me in a fiel' and I jumped up. I looked to the north, I heard a song but I didn't see nothing. [Shakes head, then points with index finger toward each direction in sequence.] I looked to the west; I didn't see nothin'; south, I didn't. When I looked to the east, three blue gate flew out the east [spreads his arms] and a light was shining on in each window coming down on me and it got nigh to me. Captain, dis what the song it was singin.'[He sings with a beautiful, steady voice in the key of D.]

"Shine on me, oh Lordy, shine on me, Let the light from the lighthou' *shine...on...me.*" [He emphasizes these last three words by prolonging the vowels and lowering his upraised palms three times].

And I jump up and a bunch of angel was be singin' this same song 'n I say, "Hol' it!" I say. [Here he sings to the tune of "Amazing Grace" while slowly moving his hands as if directing a choir.]

"When I heard this voice of Jesus say, 'Come home to me, I riz.' Oh Lord! Lie down thou [looks upward, seems to forget words] thy hea-d upon my breast. It was grace re-taught my heart to fear, and grace will lead me on. How hap-py hour thou gra-ce appear, the hour I firs' believe."

[Claps hands, then speaks rapidly.] And I got to shouting and the angel took me by the hand and carry me to the barrack and I wake up the whole company.

Flossie Sarvis Morris.

Florence "Flossie" Sarvis Morris

Born 1894

"Not drafted."

Where's "'onway"? This is my nickname for Catherine's sedan, which lacks the first letter of its trunk-decal from Conway Ford. Now the car itself is missing from the carport of 1409 Eighth Avenue. Nobody answers the doorbell next to the woodpile where I have often dropped off transcripts for correction, so she must have forgotten our appointment. I drive on alone—or, rather, with my daughter, not quite eleven years old, who has somehow mistaken my invitation for compulsion. We journey about ten miles down Highway 701 toward the southern border of the county and stop at the old house in the woods at 6400 Flossie Road. About this time, Catherine leaves our rendezvous place in the parking lot of the A&P and returns to her carport wondering what has happened to Randall and disappointed at not being able to interview a colorful icon.

Bucksville is now a notion as much as a location. But in 1883 it had seven hundred people, three churches, several private schools, two hotels and several sawmills along the Waccamaw. The chief shipping point for Conway, as well as for a large area of backcountry, it sent out naval stores, timber and cotton. A regular line of three vessels plied between this point and New York City, as did a line of schooners to Baltimore. Forty to fifty vessels carried lumber, some to the North, others to the West Indies and South America. On a list of citizens and their jobs was M.F. Sarvis, "cotton gin and civil engineer."[10]

What remains of the town and its half-mile of docks is a lone chimney, the Ozymandias of Horry. At low tide, ballast rocks emptied from ocean-going schooners can be seen on the right bank. "Miss Flossie" Sarvis Morris herself was a sort of monument; almost one hundred years old in 1991, she was a longtime teacher as well as the daughter of a Civil War veteran who had died in 1936 after living a century. Katie, the age of Flossie's first pupils almost eighty years earlier, ended up asking a few questions at Dad's behest. Unaccustomedly shy but smiling, her hair golden, she warmed the doughty woman as much as the nearby hearth.

The house, with its wooden floors and its walls of painted wood-strips, seemed to reflect the owner's interest in preserving rather than decorating. She sat in a dark wooden armchair with a floral cushion in front of loaded bookshelves and several photographs. Her arms usually folded, she wore a blue-gray dress with a white lace collar, as well as spectacles that covered alert eyes that seemed unfazed by the glare of the camera lights. Her voice was rusty yet firm, and now and then she became silent while reviewing her memory. Her mouth, creased on both sides, appeared set in a frown—until it could not keep from smiling.

My father lived here [in this community]. His father and mother lived here, and he had two brothers in the Civil War—Tenth South Carolina Volunteers—[opens eyes wide, cocks head a bit, chuckles] not drafted. And one, Uncle Joe—Joseph Asbury Sarvis—was killed at the Battle of Atlanta. Samuel Scarborough Sarvis, he was younger, was at the Battle of the Crater in Virginia [during the siege of Petersburg in 1864]. He was always very proud that he was in Lee's army. My father's general was General Bragg, and I have the book *Tenth South Carolina Volunteers* that was given to him. Colonel C.I. Walker was the colonel at the end of the war; he was from Charleston and compiled this book and sent each of the officers a bound copy, and each of the other soldiers, he gave 'em a paperbound copy.

[In the hand-colored photograph] the one nearest the fireplace is my father, Moses Floyd Sarvis, in his Confederate uniform; and the other is Joseph Asbury Sarvis. My father didn't talk about the Civil War as much as my mother did. She was a child in Chester County [in north-central South Carolina] and that's where they were looking for Sherman [the

Riverside relic of sawmill.

Union general] to pass through, but he didn't get there [laughs] because the Catawba River had overflowed. But he went through Lancaster.

My grandmother—[ponders and starts over]. My grandfather, Thomas Wade Moore, was in the seceding convention in Charleston, and he was hiding 'cause they'd 've killed him. But my grandmother took her family— her children and stepchildren—all but my mother. My mother was in with a grandmother in Chester. [Grandmother McDonald] took them and refugeed to escape Sherman, and she went right into one wing of his army. He having to change his way of getting to Chester, I reckon was reason that they got into that wing. And my grandmother was a Yankee. She was from New York. She asked the colonel or the captain to give her a guard, and he did; but they took everything they had, they had to walk back home. Sherman had eighty thousand stragglers. [Looks intently at Wells.] Part of them were Northern people, I suppose; and a lot of them were from South Carolina.

[To Katie.] Have you ever read any books about the Civil War, South Carolina? Well, let me tell you one you should read: *Another Jezebel* [Nell S. Graydon, 1958]. I'm satisfied it's in the library. She tells it in full. I'd heard my mother tell some of it.

[Laughs at question about her Yankee grandmother.] My great-grandmother was born in Pennsylvania. She was a Davis, and she married Donald McDonald, and they lived in Albany. One of the daughters had bad health—lung trouble—so they moved down to Aiken, and then they later moved to Chester. My great-grandmother kept a preparatory school for boys and girls; prepared 'em for college.

[Leaning toward Katie, now seated in a chair next to her.] I didn't understand you. [Laughs when she hears the question.] When I was about ten years old, I wore dresses. [Shakes head and looks her interlocutor in the eye with a hint of a smile.] I didn't dress like the children do now. My mother made some of my dresses and my sister made some. And I wore stockings, black stockings. If a hole came into your stocking, you had to sew that hole up; you must not show that white of your shin. [Fixes her eyes on Katie, then laughs.] I had one cousin; she was awfully smart. She got around sewing it up—by putting some smut under there, black smut [soot]. If you reach in the chimney there [laughing and pointing], you'd find some!

You want to know about going to school? Well, if I tell you too much it'll make it too long. [Laughs.] I walked to school, from down on the paved road that goes by Hebron Church—you know this little brick house out here with the chickens? Well, you don't know much about over here [laughs].

What I liked best about school was the recess. We played in the road till there was a little bit of travel. It was a dirt road; still is. There was a deep ditch, and we'd jump in da ditch and play in it, and we played in the woods. One of the chief amusements that boys had—there was a pine thicket right in front with some small pines in it. And we had a wood stove, long heaters about like that. But these boys weren't after wood. They took the axe and they went in the woods, and one boy would climb a tree, a sapling, and another boy would take the axe and cut it down, and he'd fall. [Illustrates with hand.] And then we played jump-the-rope. [Turns to Katie and laughs gently.] Have you ever played that? [Katie smiles and nods.] I was a right good jumper.

We carried our lunch in a bucket or a basket. When I was five years old I had a little tin bucket about like that [forms a small rectangle with fingers of both hands], and I carried my lunch in it. We carried lunch and ate outside. I had two sisters older than I was that were going to school, and we walked. I wasn't spoiled, but I was bad. [Deadpan stare at Katie.] After I had eaten my lunch out of the bucket, then I didn't want to carry it home. I depended on my sisters to carry it home for me. I don't know how much they did, but I wanted them to carry it home for me!

[Conspiratorially, she suppresses a smile and raises a shoulder.] I didn't do any chores if I could help it! I never did get much kick out of work. I still don't, but I've done a lot of work, though. [I started teaching] in 1913. We had to take an examination then, and I got a third-grade certificate. Well, that didn't bring in much money: that was thirty-five dollars a month. Some of them didn't even pay that, I don't think. [Chuckles.] And I started out on the Pee Dee Road in a one-teacher school. I don't know whether anyone who went to school to me is still living or not. [I quit teaching] in '56, below here, in a big brick schoolhouse.

My father liked horses. If he had a good, old, gentle horse, he'd let us drive it, but when the old, gentle horses passed on to da graveyard, we had to drive a mule. He had a fast horse but he was fractious and my father was afraid that he might hurt us—you know, or run away or something. But I think if he had let us drive the horse, we would have driven him so much till he would have tamed down.

The first steamboat on the Waccamaw was a side-wheeler [driven by a paddle-wheel on each side], the old *Elliott, George Elliott.* It carried passengers and freight to Georgetown. One day the old *Burroughs* from Conway—they met on the river. The *Burroughs* was going to Georgetown, and the *Elliott* was going back to Conway [waves hand back and forth]. Riding the boats was our way of gettin' about. The Georgetown Company had the *Sessoms*. It was a stern-wheeler [a single paddle-wheel at the stern]. It sunk down the river somewhere about Hagley [Plantation]. [Stops to ponder.] On its way back to Georgetown. They build another boat, the *Lucih V* [*Lucy V*]. I think that old Mr. John Vereen at Murrells Inlet owned a share in this company, and his daughter was named Lucy, so it was named *Lucy V.* [Long pause.] And my cousin, Frank Sarvis, was captain. He was captain on the *Sessoms*, too. They tied up at Bucksville down here at night, and the boat was burned.

The ships [schooners], when they came from the North, sailed up the river from Winyah Bay as long as they could, as long as there was wind for them to sail on. I don't think they sailed very far, though. And when the river got a little more shallow and more narrow than it was farther down, they'd—I can't tell you exactly how they did it—but anyhow, they put a man on shore and they fastened to a tree or something [gestures] and had a winch pull them up the river some. Now, you see, there's a tide [that enabled vessels to float upriver as far as Conway on the incoming tide] in the Waccamaw River; there isn't a tide in the Pee Dee. And then another way they had—they would put Nigras [Negroes] on a great big yawl boat [opens arms and extends hands], and they would pull [the vessel] up with oars. They used those boats on the rivers a lot; the fishermen used them. [Asked if she saw schooners on the Waccamaw, she searches her memory for eighteen seconds.] No. I saw sailing ships in Bull Creek. They came up to Eddy Lake to get cypress lumber to take back North.[11]

We'd listen for that [steamboat] whistle to blow; and I certainly missed the boats when they took them off [i.e., around 1920].

We went to Hebron Church, Methodist. My grandfather helped build the present building there [in 1848]. There was an old building before the present church was built. And my grandfather had a road cut straight [cuts air with hand] through his land to the church and he could walk to church.

My cousin, Lewis Beaty, was the superintendent of the Sunday school and practically ran the church. His daughter, Nanny Beaty, was a musician. We'd have an Easter program and they'd get children from all around. Some of her kin people from Murrells Inlet would come. My cousins from Socastee [across the Waccamaw via Peachtree Ferry] would come and be in it. We decorated the church up a sight. We put flowers and anything we could have. When the service closed, everybody—if they could get a handful of flowers or anything—we went out in the cemetery and put the flowers on the graves. And we sang "We Shall Sleep but Not Forever"

Florence "Flossie" Sarvis Morris

Both venerable.

and were dismissed there in the cemetery. I guess that was the outstanding thing. [Laughs gently.]

[Invited to give advice to children of Katie's age] Well, learn to say "No, thank you" and to keep your identity. Join good things like Girl Scouts and your school affairs. And read. Do you like to read? [Not satisfied.] Well, you read! Because that's most I've learned is what I've read. Church school is good. And just be good! [Laughing, she reaches over and squeezes Katie's arm.] Listen to your mother and your father. And if anybody tries to get you to do something you shouldn't do, and they call you "chicken," you'll say, "Well, I like to be a chicken." [laughs]

[In the backyard, Miss Flossie stands with the help of a cane next to a large iron cauldron, her slight lean emphasized by the vertical boards of the unpainted shed behind her.] During the Civil War they needed salt and the best way to get it was to go down to the beach and boil the salt water. And my uncle, Louis Floyd Sarvis [taps her cane on the grass], boiled salt down on the coast during the war. Also my aunt's husband, James E. Dusenbury. My father was fighting Yankees. Do you want that in? [Chuckles, eyes twinkling.]

Lillie Louise Brown Latimer and Ruth Clay Woodbury.

Liffie Louise Brown Latimer
&
Ruth Clay "Sabe" Woodbury

Born 1882 and 1886

"He died and ain't paid Grown Man a cent for burying he wife this day."

Driving slowly along Racepath Avenue in Conway, I peer out the window in search of house number 1712. No luck. So I cross Highway 501 between vehicles reluctantly halted, northbound and southbound; this was the stoplight that Reverend Dr. S. George Lovell fought to retain so as to avoid dividing the black community (see Catherine's interview of 1990). Strangely enough, the only place this address can logically designate is a big old house with plywood windows that's spooky and set back among the trees that shadow it. ("The colored section," a white person once noted with mischievous irony, "has the best live oaks in Conway.") Near the abandoned residence, a couple of men lounge on the hood of a car, no doubt looking askance at this white fellow, and a new police substation marks a rough area. So, unable to reach anyone by telephone and needing to confer about a transcription, I try plan B by driving around the corner to Highway 378 to the Latimer Funeral Home, which is owned by the descendants of the people interviewed.

That session was conducted thirty-six years earlier, on January 29, 1970, at the same 1712 Racepath Avenue, the home of Mrs. Lillie Louise Brown Latimer. She had been born in 1882, the daughter of Sarah and Thomas Brown. Also interviewed was her half-sister, Ruth Clay "Sabe" Woodbury, the daughter of Sarah Brown and Jimmy Clay. The Latimer family owned the town's first African American funeral home, founded in 1924 after Mrs. Latimer's son George, called Grown Man, went to embalming school in Raleigh. In 2006, his widow, Edna, and his son, George Jr., met with me when I showed up at the funeral home with a mysterious packet, and it wasn't long before they gave me the imprimatur for this chapter.

The original interviewers were Mrs. Catherine H. Lewis and Mrs. Etrulia P. Dozier, a librarian in the public schools and one of the few people to write about the history of African Americans in Horry County. The interview was recorded on antiquated reel-to-reel tape. Twenty years later a cassette copy was made and the first half transcribed by Ann Ipock, then most of the second half by Randall A. Wells with the help of the interviewers. In 2006 he refined the entire transcription, but many of its sounds have yet to crystallize into symbols. The tape's fidelity was not the best and it faded mysteriously at times, the half-sisters were hard to distinguish and often talked simultaneously; their English was an African-influenced variety learned 120 years earlier, children sometimes made noise in the background, the radio broadcast music or talk, the telephone rang, an adult yelled at a child, a door slammed and the clock struck eight. Nevertheless, Wells felt privileged to be an ear-witness to a bustling household of decades ago, and he grew fond of the two women being interviewed.

Latimer: I know the hotel was there when I used to tote the clothes, wash the sheets for a dollar and a half. On my head—clean from downtown. Bag come down to have twenty-one and two sheets and I'd been home washing and ironing. All day. I ran away from home and got married when I was fifteen. After I had finished high school, the people sent me to college and I run away and got married.

[The school was] in the Baptist church. Across in front of the school, they called it [where soldiers assembled for inspection] the Muster Field. And they had a shed built out there. We used to go every day at twelve o'clock and put up in there and eat what we carried to school. This same street here used to be a racetrack, and that's why they named it Racepath. They had races in the Muster Field, yes.

Woodbury: I was a child and I remember when they got on the horses and pick the thing up—catch the ring in there.

[The women talk at the same time about the number of grades in the school.]

[Identity of speaker uncertain:] About six weeks—and in this particular house, they had a first and second and third, fourth. We went as high as the seventh grade. We were graduated then. Yes, I can remember the names of some of the teachers. Used to be a Professor [Theodore] Gordon, used to work in the post office. He used to teach in that old Whittemore Schoolhouse. Just had one teacher. And they would have spelling matches about once a month and all the parents would have to go to the schools and the children all get in line and have spelling matches; as you'd spell, they'd go up. And George Singleton [b. 1894] was always one of the smartest ones in the class.

Latimer: And done away with the old schoolhouse on Racepath. And [then] it was taught in the old academa [academy]. But there was a white schoolhouse there, and the white people done away with it. They let the colored people to teach in it and that's the last school that Sabe 'n myself went to. I don't know if there is any white people that can remember that, but it used to be the white people would go—where we were over this side, they was over there.[12] They stopped teaching in that schoolhouse and turned it over to the colored people. The last teacher that we went to in that schoolhouse was J.E. Tallman.

[How did people earn a living?]
Woodbury: Old lady Mary Beaty.[13] You know where Spivey lived [at 428 Kingston, Conway, home of D.A. Spivey, mayor]? She was living in that big old house and her sister was living in the yard in that small house. And so Miz Beaty went to move off Main Street. She built a store in her yard and my father used to still for her—rawzin [rosin] still. Used to carry my father dinner and breakfast a many and many a morning and days.[14]

Latimer: Miz Beaty had a farm out there on Pee Dee [Road, which parallels the Little Pee Dee River]. A crowd over there—Elsie Woodbury and a crowd of men calling. All of them used to go every morning on that ride into that farm. That's where they lived.

Woodbury: Yes, my great-grandmama [unnamed mother of Sally Powell] used to tell us about slavery. She said she was the only child that her mother had and said used to put them on the block and sell them. And said they would save the soap, the grease out of the kitchen like we used to save to make soap grease. Like they was going to have a sale tomorrow, they would grease them up and put them on the block to sell them. They would examine them and come around and see if they wanted to buy them.

And Grandma [Martha Ann Brown] said she [the mother of Sally Powell] didn't have but one child and they sold her and carried her to Marion. And said she got so disturbed and mad up about it, she runned away and stayed in the woods six months. Said she didn't stay in the woods, said where she stayed—right in the missus's house, but they didn't know it. Said she would go in the woods all day, and at night she would be upstairs and learned how to spin cloth all day looking down at her missus. Spinning. Said the cook would slip her something to eat upstairs and at night, she'd come down. My great-grandmother is the one who said they sold her and my grandmother was a slave, but my mother wasn't.[15]

Latimer: They brought her from Bamberg [South Carolina]. Said to the Bamberg somewhere.

Woodbury: Bought the land where I am living. She bought twenty-five acres for a dollar an acre. They had to pay a dollar down and dollar a month. And the only way they could get that dollar was to make the payment—they had to split rail—ah, split shingles in the woods, or cut cordwood, something like that.

Latimer[?]: I remember it wasn't but my mother house and the old Inman house…and the John Moore house there. And Annie Johnson. And this used to be nothing but a oak ridge, oak ridge and big old high [longleaf] pines.

Woodbury: And where the hospital is [i.e., the former Conway Hospital on Ninth Ave. between Bell and Buck Streets], that used to be the Hamm Pond [rhymes with "loaned"].

Latimer[?]: The boys would go swimming—get naked and go right in. [Laughs.] Go right where the hospital is built now. All that was thick woods.
Woodbury: Well, there were plenty of Negroes [she makes an exclamation that sounds like the French "quoi"], but seemed to me like they didn't know nothing but the farm. They never did make me farm much. My mother didn't have anybody but me. And that wouldn't make me work [?] and my

great-grandma [Sally Powell] was a midwife. She used to massage them and they'd give her three dollars to get the baby [?]. [Laughter.]

Latimer: Yes, before the funeral homes, all the thing they did was just to run along with Frank Brown and bury them. Put ice and salt on you.

Woodbury: Like somebody was dead here tonight, the house would be full directly. Well, they'd cook and eat, sing and shout all night. Just wash them and dress them and lay 'em out on a board. Cover them up with a sheet in the house. That where they kept them till the time they buried them and then they would carry them in the wagon to the graveyard. Right there by Bethel Church. It's been so long. [The monuments] all rotted down. I saw one of the tombstones leaning. My brother Henry. Cousin Lillie. When the church was smaller, come a storm and the church blowed down. They propped it up with pine boards.

Latimer: [As for rural churches,] I know they used to go to Bucksport [just downstream from Bucksville] and have big meetings. They had one on the other side of the campground out on—they call it Sand Ridge now. We didn't have a wharf. When the boats run, you'd have to tie the boat to a cypress knee. You'd get way up there and tie the boat. Them passengers they'd put boards and sometimes you'd have to take off shoes and wade to get off the boat.

Woodbury: Yes, my Uncle Sammy [worked on a river boat]. Used to be engineer. It was the *Burroughs* and the *Maggie*, wasn't it, Lillie? And the *Ruth* kept him busy. Down there turning the wheel. Yes [I traveled on one of those boats]. Mmmm, mmm! Was the happiest night of my life! When time for the excursion. We didn't have any music and they had a band. And when the band started blowing and excursion going tomorrow, ooh!

Latimer: That's the only way we could get to Georgetown. We'd go on excursion on Fridays and Saturdays. Friday night, not Saturday.

Woodbury: And my mama used to run a table. She'd cook all that good stuff and—say we going tomorrow, she'd cook all day today. And used to come crackers in little boxes and she'd fry that box full of fish, then fry another one. She'd have another 'n for the [?] cook it. Then she'd put the stove on the boat and have the grease fried hot. And then the people— didn't have a whole lot of stuff—they'd buy then. Give ten or fifteen cent

47

Mitchelle C.

piece, twenty cent pliece [piece]. And she'd be sold out all that food, going to Georgetown. Got down there, she'd have to buy more and cook all the way back.

Latimer: In Georgetown we went to the Candy Kitchen. My aunt wouldn't have no quarter. And get a nickel's worth of taffy candy and nickel of this, spend all over my dime. Come back to the boat.

Woodbury: What time, Lillie?

Latimer: Get there about twelve o'clock.

Woodbury: We'd get there about twelve o'clock and then we'd dress. We'd carry our clothes like we were going on excursion, wouldn't dress up. We carried a basket and just about the time—everybody would be running to put on their dress. Go up the streets in Georgetown. And went down with that quarter. The band would dance on the head of the boat all the way down and all the way back. No, preachers didn't [try to keep us from dancing]. They would go, but they didn't dance. We used to sit in the living room upstairs [where] some of the people didn't even see them dance. I'd love to see 'em dance. I'd have been out there, but my mother wouldn't let me go and I had to sit near that table where she was sellin'.

Then we used to go on the train when it used to run right down Main Street. We'd go to the lake [Lake Waccamaw in North Carolina, origin of the river]. What time did we go? I believe at six. Charter a train to go. From the depot where Mr. McKeithan house was right there. That's where the turntable used to be. No, the turntable up there by George Dusenbury house. That's where the Epps boy got killed.

Yes, all the white ladies was always nice to us and Gamma and them. ["Gamma" is pronounced with a nasalized final syllable rather like the French "gamin."] Mr. Causey had his place down here by me. His daddy used to bring Gamma loads of wood for fifty cents in the mule and wagon. And then on Saturday, sometimes he'd bring a load of watermelons for Gamma and them to sell on Sunday and they'd sell them for five or ten cents. And Monday Mr. Causey daddy come and Gamma would have a dollar and a half for him. Sometimes he'd give them fifty cents for selling them. Sometimes if we didn't have nothing else, they'd bring corn or something that they had. That was the only way they had food. Used to make all the food. Used to plant our rice patch right where the motel is now. The place was damp down there.

Well, I think [people got land] for little or nothing, 'cause they [the Negroes] didn't know any better. Uncle Israel Davis—there wasn't a soul in the world but Dr. Norton. [Either J.A. Norton, 1876–1950, or Evan Norton, 1841–1914). Old man, Dr. Norton. If he had any money, he carried it Dr. Norton to keep. [Laughs.] If he got fifty cents, he carried it with Dr. Norton. Then he died. [Aunt] Annie didn't know nothing 'bout what he had, 'cause he didn't ever give her his money. So they got the land mixed up right in there. Some of the older ones come here and tried to get it straight but they couldn't. So then the Hollidays got it. And that's from Front Street all the way over to the A&P store [1302 Fourth Avenue]. 'Cross from there used to be our land.

Latimer: Grandma said she had to wrop me up and wrop her [Ruth] up to bring me from downtown because that's when the earthquake was.[16] Said Sarah hadn't been outdoor—you know, we'd be staying in the house three weeks when they have a baby. And you couldn't wash your [the baby's] feet in a month. [Laughter.] Had a white spigot, wipe his feet.

[Catherine asks about places of residence and about Negro businesspeople.]
Woodbury: I remember my mama used to cook for Miz Nolley. [Mr. E.W. Nolley was the editor of the *Horry Herald*.] I was a child. They used to cook the sweet biscuits that day and gimme one of them. Oh, I'd be so tickled. And Janie Newton used to run a restaurant right along where Solomon Brothers' store is. Mollie house…remember that, Lillie? And Liza Malloy lived in the back of where their house is. She owned all of that—tobacco warehouse right in front of the Red & White. And Aunt Jane lived across the street; colored people lived there. And Aunt Jane runned the business, the restaurant.

Mollie Johnson didn't work—all she done was set with Mary [Beaty] all the time. She was doing everything you say, well, "Ask Miss Mary," "Tell Miss Mary 'bout it." And Uncle Tom, her [Lillie's] daddy, was working at the store and deek out [hand items to people from behind the counter] of everything. Wait on the people. He was the head man around the yard. On Saturday he was the one would wait on 'em—used to weigh out, what to buy. And Uncle Thomas would be down here to—tend to all Miss Mary business.

Latimer: [Later] my father was a caulker; he caulked boats. The *Maggie*, the *Burroughs*, and all those boat people. Down at Georgetown. My step-daddy [Jimmy Clay] where the depot is now on the boat. And my father used to work on the boats where—"The Shipyard." Over the bridge where all those oak trees is [near Kingston Presbyterian Church.] [Then] he went into preachin'.

[Discussion of Negro leaders, male and female.]
Woodbury: Reverend Wilson and my mother—the only one that had any boarders. My mama cousin, Sarah Wilson. And Sally Powell, them were the only midwife. She made all the money, give 'em three dollars for a baby. [To Lillie:] What that name? His wife was Carrie downtown—oh, she run the place where they sell cotton, clothing—Mr. Edwards. Gamma used to go out three miles down there riding on horseback for his wife, and he'd give her a ham every time she go and add three dollars.

Latimer: And old man Bob Brown, my granddaddy, used to walk from here to Georgetown. All the time. He run the flat. That's the only way they got fertilizer. He would go to Georgetown and get 'em rollin'. And have his hands that polled [pulled?] in the river and flat's up and he'd put them to come and he'd walk from Georgetown to Conway. And cut 'em off. One time they said Papa found—the mailman lost a sack of money and said he finally brought it back to Mr. Burroughs. Said Mr. Burroughs gave him a dollar. [Laughs.]

Woodbury: Mr. Burroughs was good to me. Sent me a box of groceries—turkey settin' on top of it—every Christmas.[17] Yeah, I went to that [the lurid murder trial of Edmund Bigham of Pamplico, held at the Horry County Courthouse in 1924[18]]. Old lady [?] Johnson and myself we'd go every day. Roasted a potato or baked one and carry it—so we wouldn't have to get up. The courthouse would be so full, we couldn't move. Because the people from Bigham then stayed at my house that night, the ones that come to the trial. The courthouse was so full of people that we couldn't get a seat and wouldn't get up till court adjourned.

[Subject changes again.]
Latimer: The year of the shock [earthquake]—I was big enough to know that something was happening, but I didn't know what it was, and I wasn't afraid of it. My mother was in the house with some other children, and she couldn't get out. People used to come at night and bring their children here and they all would go to church.

Woodbury: What Mary [?] told me, she was like Lillie; what she said she could remember they cooked some backbone and rice together and they had the sweetener and they didn't have stove. They put the pot under the table on some sand. Mary said everybody went to hollerin', and she slipped under the table and went to eatin' out of the pot with her hands. Peter, her daddy—when they started to go to church everybody run to church to pray, "Oh-h, Lord! Where me child?" Pulled her out from under the table, when she got to church she had her hands full of that rice. [Laughter.] People were singin' 'n shoutin'.

[General discussion and joviality. Subject turns to Hurricane Hazel, 1954.]
Woodbury: I remember the bishop and his secretary and his chauffeur was stopping here with us. Grown Man had just built that house, and he come in here and say, "Oh, I declare, Atlantic Beach ain't nothin'—all those houses gone or if they don't they be settin' in the middle of the street!"

[More prominent local African Americans are recalled. One is Lawrence Hemingway, who became a bishop in the AME (African Methodist Episcopal) Church. Another is George Singleton, editor of the *Christian Recorder* and author of an autobiography, who was "one of our men that we could feel proud of."[19] Mrs. Dozier then asks about the funeral business.]

Woodbury: The first funeral home we had was right here in this yard. Right there by that oak tree's be sittin' there. And we built a hall over the funeral home and you'd have parties 'n things in the hall.

Latimer: I know this old man that's dead right now that married Mary mama. Wasn't he a [last name]? Grown Man bury wife for him time of the flu. Every time Grown Man go out there to get the man after his money, he'd run and hide around the house. And Grown Man would catch him, and he'd say [imitates a huffing man], "Well you know we had that flu, we had that flu." And he died and ain't paid Grown Man a cent for burying he wife this day and he's dead and buried now.

I remember he [Mr. Gordon, postmaster and teacher] was very strict. Every Monday when we went to school, everybody had to explain what happened yesterday. Or if you wasn't in Sunday school, why wasn't you in Sunday school and why wasn't you in church. And we couldn't say, oh, dis 'n dat, all kind o' words. And Orrin Mack? He was tryin' to speak proper, speak like a teacher, and went to the post office one day—it was just a little hole. [Loudly] "Is there any mail here for I?" [Laughter.]

[Catherine asks about religious, civic and fraternal organizations.]
Latimer: Yeah, I know somethin' about them now. We had—way back—had a Oddfellows Lodge. Old man Allen Parmley and who else…Henry Jones, Bob Brown, old man Thomas Brown, my daddy. Now you come to the Good Samaritans; my daddy was the grand chief of the Good Samaritans. [The ladies cannot remember the years.]

Woodbury: And the Daughters of Ruth. That was also the Oddfellows. I don't think we have over twenty-five. 'Long in there—now we used to have crowds 'n crowds—they fell out. Some of 'em dead 'n some just got slack.

Latimer: It was along there in 1925 'n '26. [As an organization we would] pay so much to bury the dead and pay so much when you're sick and pay so much—ran offices. [As for orphans,] it was like somebody give they child to somebody who was able to take care of it. Remember Aunt Lillie gave 'em all to Gamma. Her mother died and wasn't able to take care of her. That's the way we used to do. [Social problems were] all taken care of within the various families in the community.

Woodbury: The only way—if you were sick, we might give a nickel to give you or carry a little rice, or a little piece of meat or somethin'. And then on Sundays, we'd go to carry 'em some dinner. And so when these little organizations come along, payin' you a dollar a week or somethin', that was big money.

[After a discussion of the first Negroes to go away to college, Ms. Dozier asks about lynchings.]
[**Speaker unclear**:] Oh, Gamma would tell us—people used to say they would do, but there wasn't anything like that going on.

Woodbury: Like everybody was friendly. [Lively discussion.] We never had any trouble here. Other than that I got along with everybody. Everybody respected me and I respected them. Now you take Mary Bell. [?] My husband didn't want me to do it, wouldn't let him know I was washing and ironing for them. But I slipped [worked clandestinely—V. Gerald] and washed for them people until them children are got grown. And they were just as nice to me—. I saw Mary and old man Tom down to Bucksport about a year before she died. And oh, they were so glad to see me. We went down there to buy some shad [a fish that ascends rivers from the sea in order to breed]. One year I hadn't paid my tax. It was a time way up in April. "Sabe"—he called me "Sabe," my nickname—"I hear that you ain't paid—your husband hasn't paid your tax, what's the matter, you need some assistance?" They would respect me, treated me nice, talk 'n laugh 'n shake hands with me. [Animated discussion.] Not like the things going on like you carryin' on now.

Latimer: I went to Mary Bell over there, "Lillie, you've got to come in and have some dinner, you've just got to"—something like that before dinner sometimes. I've always got along…and I don't know why. I think it's a matter of foolishness. I don't think it's a bit of need of it.

Woodbury: Tommy Bellamy would have fish fries. Like we gon' have a fish fry tomorrow, he'd come by tonight, "Y'all be at my yard?" Fish fry in the mornin' and when we'd go to the river—we'd go down on the other side of the big mill [Conway Lumber Company on the Waccamaw]—and we'd get to the river, come down we'd done have two tubs of fish caught. And we'd stay down there, crowds of us, and he'd feed us fish. He wouldn't charge anything, all you'd do is carry him a piece of ice and have some ice water. We'd make lemonade, a barrel o' lemonade. Oh-h, we could have the biggest time. And some of the white people'd be with us. [Volume fades.] But that was some of our biggest time in Conway, wouldn't we, Lillie—eat all the fish you want. Some of them would be big old fish. Stay down there all day.

[Catherine asks about courting customs.]
Woodbury: I runned away 'n got married, wouldn't let me court. My mother never would allow me to have company. The man I married, I would write notes and send 'em by John Moore. He'd write a letter back to me and send it by John. And one day Marvin [her boyfriend and future husband] wrote me a letter to give it to Aunt Betsy. And Aunt Betsy, 'stead of givin' me the letter she gave it to Sarah. My Mama and Sarah wore me out. This love letter he had give me. So Miss Jane [?], Marguerite mama, told me [?].

We dug a deep hole—like we had to jump over the fence there in the country—'n put some corn stalks over it and then put some sand over it, and straw. And Aunt Betsy come home that night she jumped over that fence [laughter]. [?] Broke her hip. [Consternation and laughter.] Nobody didn't never know—Miss Jane told me last year [?]. Tellin' on you that you got that letter from Marvin. That's why I runned away got married—I couldn't go with no boys. I had to stay home.

[This audiocassette ends. It is a partial copy of the original reel-to-reel tape, whereabouts unknown. On a second cassette the author discovered the ending of the original tucked away somewhere, still un-transcribed for lack of time.]

Woodrow W. Long.

Woodrow W. Long

Born 1913

"And then the last bucket they'd pull me up with it."

Rounding a curve on Long Avenue Extension, you cross the bridge over Crabtree Swamp and come upon a field to the right, an oasis of farmland just to the north of Conway. Until a few years ago you might have seen a man in a lightweight pith helmet striding toward a barn with his dog trotting nearby. This was Mr. Woodrow Long, a retired rural mail carrier and former neighbor of the author, who described him in *Along the Waccamaw*. Gentle and thoughtful, Mr. Long appreciated the author's enjoyment of the farm and its attendant novelties like milo grain, a potato bank and bovine opera.

In 2006 his widow, Dorethea, explained that Woodrow grew up in the Depression and had no opportunity for higher education. "Family responsibilities always took his time and effort, but he made the most of his circumstances without complaints."

The first of three interviews took place in March of 1990, across the road from his home at 104 Country Club Drive. Bespectacled, his shirt a lighter blue than the sky, Woodrow tucked his hat under his arm to reveal bushy white hair. During the first part of the interview, the two faced each other while leaning their arms on a gate. Behind the barbed wire a half dozen brown cows wandered in and out of the videotape by mass, muzzle, ear and tail. Behind the herd stood an unpainted gray tobacco barn with its metal skirts, and behind that the field sloped toward gray-bark wetlands. Tall pines cast shifting, dappled shadows on the two men, and a few times the triadic blast of an air-horn could be heard as a train poked through North Conway on the single track.

I believe my great-grandfather bought this land about 1848. At five and a half acres, I usually grow the grain that I feed my cows with and my horse. This is my garden spot over to the right, and then I have another part of the land that you do not see from here, and it also serves as a pasture in the summertime. I believe you are familiar with that with your walking years ago. [Points.] That's the conjunction of Kingston Lake [Swamp, a major tributary of the Waccamaw], Brown Swamp and Crabtree Swamp. I believe my granddaddy worked in town at one time. He had a job at the courthouse, and he paddled a boat down Kingston Lake to town part of the time. There just wasn't any roads—nothing but footpaths, no bridges—so a boat was about the only thing they got to cross the water with.

Two brothers, my Uncle Hamp [Jabez Hampton Long] and my father [William Mack Long, 1881–1954], inherited a strip of land—each one, one on the north side of Brown Swamp and one on the south side. The others [i.e., pieces of land] got out of the family years ago.[20] My grandfather was in the army of Tennessee with General [Joseph E.] Johnston. He took a fever, and they finally told him that he was going to die and that if he wanted to try to come home, he could try. So he started and met a man with a wagon coming to Cherry Grove Beach to get salt. You know, the Yankees had captured Vicksburg, which cut us off from the salt mines in Louisiana. That's how desperate it was. For years I could not believe that story that a man from Arkansas would come to get salt all the way to the ocean. But my grandfather rode with him, and when he got home, he recuperated well in Horry County. So he went down to Georgetown and volunteered for that coastal defense battery—Belle Isle, I believe—and ended the war there. That also ended the plantation and all that. Family inheritance, as it was known then, became a kind of survival test of those who could.

Yes [they owned slaves]. They paid nine hundred dollars for the one thousand one hundred acres of land in this area. [Points in various directions:] It extended from that big old oak tree in Snow Hill Field out to Homewood and then over to Kingston Lake [where Kingston Lake Swamp widens near downtown Conway] and then back through here. They only paid nine hundred dollars for it, but they paid one thousand for each male slave, and they had bought several. They paid cash for the land and mortgaged the land to buy slaves. In less than [twenty] years, the slaves were free, so they lost the land. It's a fact of life. It did cause hardships, but every good thing comes through pain, doesn't it? [Smiles and nods.] They were still proud. My father was proud of this land and he wanted us to keep it. He wanted us to live on it, so most of us have.

My great-grandfather [Isaac G. Long, 1810-1886], when his wife died, he had trouble with this land; I guess he was ready to give it up. It so happened that he went to Toddville [south of Conway] and married a widow lady [Ingabo B. Gore], and she had land, so he, in a way, did not feel too lost about losing this. My grandfather, he stayed here till his first wife died. She was buried on the farm.[21]

They [my great grandfather and his second wife] were buried in Union Church Cemetery. My grandfather went to Maple [a few miles north of Conway] and married a Thompson, where she owned a lot of land, so they kind of set up an estate there. So my grandfather was not on Long land when he died, and he was buried on his wife's property. His children stayed up there a long time. In a way that was home. That's when I [went to] school in the country: that's where it was, at Maple, until I was in the third grade. My father ended up with eleven children—he had about eight at the time—and decided if they wanted a better school or to have any chance of an education, he'd better get closer to a good school. So he moved and built this place for his children to go to school at Conway. I guess we reclaimed the old place then, which is originally Long land, but Maple is our church. It's almost a hundred years old.

[Wells asks about his grandmother, Eliza Thompson Long, 1851–1928, a friend of a slave girl who was freed early.] I remember several things. One was the faithfulness of the visit [during World War I and into the 1920s]. Once a week, she would come. It was more like two long-lost friends that just met for the first time, and they would talk, talk, talk and share with each other all day long. They seemed to enjoy everything they did.

And she was so old until she went barefoot and her feet were almost turned over [holds a flattened and tilted hand]. It was almost like she was walking on just pads rather than a foot. It just deformed in some way. I imagine, after she made her six billionth step, it might have gotten a little worn anyway, don't you think? She was an *elderly* person, and my grandmother was in her seventies or eighties, I guess. At the end of the day my grandmother, she would have gone through the smokehouse for a piece of meat and to the potato bank [sweet potatoes piled under a cover of earth] for some potatoes, to the meal barrel for some meal. When she left, she'd have kind of a little tote bag with a place for your arm to go through; and she'd kind of hold it up to her breast and take it home. [Crooks arm and presses it against his chest.] And she was walking about five miles to get home, but they didn't mind that. They walked; we walked.

[She lived in a house on what became Conway Golf Course, across from 2804 Graham Road.] She would walk through the swamp. There was a foot-log we'd call the Aunt Charity Foot-log. If she wasn't named that, she really lived it out as Aunt Charity. My brother and I would go to that house when we were gathering up the sheep or the cows sometimes. On the wall would be the *Charleston Mercury* paper. They pasted the wall with newspapers [for insulation]. If I'd have took the wall down and preserved it, I would have had it in a museum today. It was just an everyday occurrence at the time.

I've been stationed in [Rantoul,] Illinois, where I'd meet with people on Sundays and week time during the war, and they all had a factory job and a farm. They could do it good because they either had 80 acres or 160 acres or 320. But here, these people carved out their little farms right out of the woods. They grew cowpeas [a vine grown in the South that bears long pods with edible, pea-like seeds eaten by animals and humans] and potatoes and corn. If they got enough to survive on with what meat they could get out of the wildlife, it really was they just carved it out of the wilderness. I couldn't survive on the farm, but I wouldn't survive without it. If I sat down without working I don't believe I'd o' been here today.

[After a tour of the swamp, Woodrow records some memories it evokes.] Crabtree Swamp originates across Highway 501 almost up to Highway 378. It comes by North Conway out at the [tobacco] warehouses and the feed mill, and on down to here where it meets Kingston Lake just below us now. These trees here, I guess, were in the bottom of this wet place and nobody was able to cut them with the equipment they had at that time— with the log cart and a mule team. So they stayed there until now you see them there. They're too old now for anything but for to look at as history. I guess they might have been there when Columbus came over.

The largest one that I ever remember down here was one almost twice as big as this one [the remaining bottom half of a cypress, twice as thick as any other tree in the swamp, a once-living parallel to the old chimney at Bucksville]. All the boys would get in there and make out like they were in an Indian teepee and livin' as primitive people, or hunters out waiting for game to come by or waiting for the Indians to come through and shoot them.

[The interview resumes in an area where a few grave markers stick out from dry leaves upon which trees cast long shadows. One of the tombstones, in three fragments atop each other, reads "Charles Gore." Woodrow walks through the place holding a microphone.] This is the old Long Cemetery. My grandmother's tombstone was in the cemetery at one time, but either it's been covered up by a tree or it's disappeared. Now you see the indentures here. The soil is elevated but it's still this good, heavy loam, so every grave shows still intact. And we see that there are lots of children here. That was commonplace in those days because diphtheria and smallpox and pneumonia all were considered fatal diseases, for the most part. This is the side of the cemetery in which the slaves were buried, and they seemed to have the same problems that the whites did in that they have lots of baby graves, too. But here seems to be a whole family lined up. It might have been smallpox that destroyed the whole family.

I guess Hugo [the hurricane of 1989] has dropped a lot of debris that we really need to clean off soon. Here are graves that seem to be side by side for quite a way. Here also are two wooden markers [posts about one yard high] that have been here a long time. A post could have been replaced by kindred, but it's not hardly possible because most of them began to leave this part of the country. I don't know any of the Gores that are anywhere in the community. The graves are almost like they were when the people were buried. It's kind of sad to say that maybe trees have covered up some of the graves since they've had a hundred years to grow. They could have grown into a grown tree and be blown over by a storm or lightning and then deteriorate—be completely gone without us ever seeing those trees. This cemetery seems to grow on you as being something very old and very peaceful. I hope the people who are buried here are resting and sleeping well.

[Fourteen months later, on May 8, 1991, Wells interviewed Mr. Long back at the farm, partly because the audio of the first interview had been compromised by wind.]

Kingston Lake [Swamp] reaches on up here down at this bridge [east of the farm toward Langston Baptist Church] and goes on up twelve or fifteen miles on out in the territory past Good Hope, New Home and almost up to Simpson Creek. I guess that would be the dividing line between Simpson Creek going to the Waccamaw [points in both directions] and the head of

Kingston Lake coming down through here to Conway before it gets to the Waccamaw. [There will be] a run crooked through the swamp. And then it will come to a lake, almost like a man-made lake—much wider than the other and maybe a head to it, like it might have extended on through and then the current cut the channel off and it cut in at another place and left a kind of eddy up there.

[They discuss his trip up this swamp with Miss Evelyn Snider, beginning from the lake below her ancestral home, so as to record the names of its segments.] The first lake above the Conway trestle of the railroad they call Durant Lake. Mr. Durant ["DOO-rant"] was one of the first owners of land in the Conway—Kingston Township or whatever they called it at that time. And the next point of reference was—they called it Rattlers Pond. Could have been snakes—it might've been something else. Then you come up to what we called Pewter's Point. They called it "Pint." The legend says that a chinaware salesman came to Conway or came up the river on a boat and then was coming on up as far as he could contacting prospective customers to sell chinaware. And when he got to that corner, which was sharp and the current was stronger than usual—cut there and turned him over, so the chinaware is down in that creek. The next lake we come to is Camp Lake, which is the one by Eugene Dorman's place. Then Smith Lake, which is the foot of Sherwood Drive. And then we come to Cross's Lake, which is over there on part of this land. And from there it reaches on out by the Long farm, by Maple, through the New Home section and on up farther.

Yes, it was said that my grandfather [John R. Long, 1839–1919] worked in town some, and his brother was the probate judge for a good long time. And many times when the water was up where they'd have to ford Brown [Creek] Swamp here and Crabtree there and be in mud in between, they'd merely paddle down the river, creek, Kingston Lake to Conway. And then they would do their day's work and come back. But the main reason they used the lake was for logs. Hauling logs was a real chore: roads were rough and muddy, and the logs were heavy, and the teams had been worked on farms all year, so any way they could get them there without just dead pulling them with mules, they did it.

So they would pull them to the nearest creek that had water—usually what we called a landing here or Smith Lake there—and they'd roll 'em into the creek and raft 'em. They put beams across the front and back and drive pegs through the beam into the log and tie 'em together. They would put about eight logs, if they were not too large, side b' side. Then they would do another one the same way. They'd put a coupling between the two until they had maybe a raft of logs [i.e., a chain of rafts] two hundred yards, three hundred yards long, take that all the way to Conway. So they saved a lot of trips that way.

Oh, I helped do it. But my father was a good woodsman. He could make the little square coupling. It would have to fit the hole, and the auger was one size. The little pin had to be just enough resistance to hold [jabs index finger downward] but easy enough to drive, see. So he could do that offhand with an axe without any problem at all. And then he'd push 'em out in the water, and the owners would usually get on them. They'd have a long pole, and they'd pole them down the river.

Yes, I've sawed logs. Two-man saw. And crosstie cutting; that was a job then. You could saw ties and put them out on any crossing where the railroad passed and stack them up there. Once a month the inspector, buyer, from the railroad company out of Wilmington, usually—maybe the ACL [Atlantic Coast Line] had one out of Florence, but I believe Seaboard's was in Wilmington. When the man would come along, he would tally them up and the company would mail you a check.

A lot of accidents happened to a lot of people, but as far as I know, nothing ever happened to any of the Long family of ever cutting trees. My daddy would cut his foot sometimes. He would cut with all of his might on a crosstie. You see, he had to shape that crosstie by hand with a broadaxe, which was about this broad, which would make for less licks.[22] But it was harder to control because the blade would come up nearer to your foot than you would think it would with the handle. He could make a crosstie just about as pretty as you could've sawed one and planed it off with a machine. And they all had to be, I believe, seven by twelve [inches at the ends], something like that.

Some of us fell in the river sometimes [chuckles] when we were going down; and one time there was ice on the water, but we got out and got all right, no problem. I was big enough to either carry the kerosene can that sprayed the saw to keep the turpentime [turpentine, the sticky resin] off it so it could go through the log, or carry the water jug or something when I was five, six, seven years old. I stayed in touch with the work goin' on all that time, so later I was able to saw with my brother. We doubled on one side of the crosscut saw—there were two handles standing up like this [raises fists in air, then pulls them back and forth]—and pull it from one side to the other. Well, the two of us were no match for our dad. But we tried, and he put along with us. By the way, sawing that log like this, your pull would be there. [He crouches and faces the side of an imaginary blade, then moves it left and right rather than forward and back.] But

Two-man saw, one man high.

you'd have to face the saw to keep it from going this way [from buckling, evidently]. And doing that thing day in and day out, I guess, must have made our backs a little more durable than usual.

Logging was a mainstay of the economy. It paid the taxes. My uncle's boy was the first one that went to college from this area, and he went on money from logs after they laid by the corn. You know what "laid by—" After you stopped plowing the corn, between that time and when it matured and you gathered it in. Well, we had to contend with grass then almost a whole year because we had no weed control and had no big cultivators that would really tear it up; so with just a mule, plow and all, they fought grass pretty hard through the cultivating season.

[Five days later, Wells returned for a follow-up interview under a peach tree, which led him to mention such a tree at the home of Andrew Stanley, who appears in Chapter Ten.] I hadn't thought about it until you mentioned how old his was; but I suppose pear trees are the oldest and most durable fruit tree that we have in Horry County. Because when I was a boy, every household had a pear tree, a grapevine, a cane patch—a sugar cane patch—a garden, apples, two or three kinds of apples, canning apples and early June apples for eating, and peaches also.

But as the years went by, different diseases came about and a parasite just killed the sugar cane. It got so small it just didn't grow knee high, so everybody just quit. It just died, that's all. And the fruit trees—people have to replant or start over pretty regularly because of the diseases that come. Grapes were put up as preserves, and some people were known to make wine out of them, too. [Smiles.] Most children ate them right off the vine. And they were good, too. I believe that's about the history of the fruit in Horry. People are going back into more of it because we have better spraying systems and more insecticides for the pests that come along.

Only Daddy had a pocketknife in our family until the boys got up pretty big age, and a pocketknife was considered a little dangerous. They kept them sharp because they had to use them for a lot of different things. So when we went to the cane patch, we usually went on our own and peeled our cane with our teeth [chuckles] and chewed it with our teeth. And I guess that's why at seventy-eight I still have all my teeth and haven't been to the dentist now in two or three years. Some good comes out of every hardship, I guess.

We had a surface well in the front yard, and about the last thing I remember about the well was they sent me down to bucket, to dip the dirt, and then they'd pull it up, you see, to make a cleanout. When a dry spell would come, the well would get fairly near dry or some would dry up; and rather than let them dry up, they'd try to clean it out and dig it a little deeper. So I went down in the well on the rope—I guess I was the lightest one and the smallest one—and would fill the bucket and they'd pull it up, and then the last bucket they'd pull me up with it. There's eleven children in the family—five of them had white teeth from the surface water of the well. When we moved down here, we had an artesian well [i.e., we drilled to a deep source of water, which had excessive fluoride] and then that began the mottled teeth like is characteristic of Horry County—our teeth were, too.

[How was the original Long tract split up?]

My great-grandfather first gave it to two of his sons, and I hadn't thought about it before. Then my grandfather gave it to two of his sons. After the Civil War the land was almost worthless. The occupation forces forced such high taxes on it to pay for the indemnity that was assessed against the Southern states. The taxes were so high that they were not able to pay them because the sources of income was all cut off practically and unless somebody was fortunate enough to have some outside income or relatives with income outside of this area, it was just about impossible to make a go of it.

[Yes,] they forfeited the land. Probably in one way deserving so in that they had invested it in slaves, but that was counted the thing to do at that time. But we know now that it was wrong, so I have no regrets about what might have been. It doesn't matter to me. We might be great landowners now instead of just a few acres [smiles] if we had not had the unfortunate— or fortunate—matter of losing or having to give up the slaves.[23]

Link Vereen.

Link Vereen

Born approx. 1889

"And I'd get on my knees and I'd take my axe and I'd cut that tree."

L ooking up from my magazine at the dentist's office, I notice that an elderly man is making his way out with the help of a cane. This is the same person I'd seen while we filled jugs of defluoridated water at a public facility in Conway. Would this stranger be a candidate for an interview? A willing one? Would an ambush be professional? On the sidewalk I catch up with him, introduce myself, venture to make the request and hear the response, "I guess so."

Link Vereen, alias Donnie Grant, turned out to be the same person that Catherine had tried to interview on behalf of the historical society after discovering that he had registered for service in World War I. (Although he gave his year of birth as 1884, many people back then reckoned it as 1888 or 1889, which would make him about the same age as Dave Carr. Many people back in time had only a rough idea of their birth year, and the author dates Link's as closer to 1888, close to Dave Carr's.) In 1991, she made another try along with the director and David Parker, videographer. They drove down Highway 90, turned right onto International Drive (grandiose name for an unpaved road), turned into the yard and parked near his car and his junked rowboat against which leaned a tire and sledge hammer. His modest house was shaded by a large oak.

The interviewee sat below a shelf that held an elaborate clock and two framed photographs of family members. Other photographs were taped to a wall that needed a fresh coat of white paint. His large armchair was vinyl—brown, white and cream. A trim, bald man, Link wore glasses; a light pink, short-sleeved shirt that sharply contrasted with his dark skin; gray pants; and white socks without shoes. One ear was scalloped by what he said was a windshield in an automobile wreck, one eyelid sagged a bit and his lips lacked full mobility, a touch that emphasized his generally unsmiling demeanor. Looking at the floor most of the time as if in thought, he spoke slowly with a rather deep voice, prolonging his vowels like a singer. Although he would often pause in thought, he could also shoot back an answer almost before the question had ended. Courteous but self-possessed, he once repeated something to Catherine with more volume than patience as if she were the one hard of hearing. He gestured frequently, often with a piece of folded white paper. Catherine, the main interviewer, sat close enough to him to put her hand on the front of the chair's wide arm.

Some months later, Wells returned, by appointment, to obtain the interviewee's signature on release forms for tape and transcript. When nobody answered the door, he enlisted the old man's nephew, who pounded on the house and woke him up. Vereen (who had the reputation as a rough young man) emerged vexed and, furthermore, determined not to sign the forms: "You could take my house." On another day, a neighboring relative secured a verbal okay. The author thanks Onetta H. Deas for reviewing an earlier version of this chapter.

I know what the Bible teaches us is "Do unto others as you wish to be done unto—[suddenly forte] that your days may be long upon the land which the Lord thy God giveth thee." I've never been an—ownlewdy [unruly (suggested by A.W. Vasaune)] boy and I'm 107 years old, and I never been in no prison. And I never will of have been to court one time. I've never been no jailhouse bird [nods head to emphasize syllables]. And I've tried to serve the Lord, and I've tried to tell people just things that I thought would do them good. And days they'd come and then day's they'd passed. *Some* believed and some didn't. [Nods head slightly a few times.][24]

I was born right back up there, I reckon about a mile from here. There's a man that owned Reaves Ferry, Bill Reaves [1853–1923]. And I was a little o' boy, I'd run around there and he'd give me crackers and candy. People would come and holler and want to go across the river; I'd put 'em 'cross. Sometimes I'd take the boat and go across and get them, and if it took a cart, mule or oxens, something like that, I'd take the flat. [Pauses.] Pull *hit* 'cross.

And then after I got man enough or big enough to get out on a permanent job, I went to work over here at th' Allentown [now-defunct site of a lumber operation north of Conway]. And I'd go 'cross down there at night and on the weekend I'd come home. That Sunday evenin', I'd go back across there going back to my job. We'd cross the Waccamaw—you know where Hickory Grove is? All right, we'd go right out there and take that right kind of road there, go on across the swamp and go out into Allen.

There was a man, foreman, by the name of George Byrd [who arrived in 1907]. He kinda liked me, and he'd take me onto an old lever car he had. He'd run up and down the railroad [waves hand]. He said, "Donnie," he'd say, "you set right here and put your foots over here. You won't get hurt." And I'd sit up there and I'd ride all day with him, and me and him would talk.

And so after then, I went to the team crew and they give me a pair of mules. The bossman told me, "Now," say, "I want to learn you how to be a driver." He said, "We're not looking for you to pull logs like the rest of these old, you see, but you just take these mules and pit up and down the road, and when you can pull a log, pull a log." I took them mules and I started out and I saw that I was man enough to holler at them [laughs]. And I put them mules to work and I'd go there and bring in just as many logs as the rest of them would. They'd made a lot of my-ration [admiration] at me, and I drove wagon until I learnt how to do that good.

Then they tuck me from there and they put me to a skidder to top-load the cars. A skidder is a machine that had a tree—a big, high tree [like a telephone pole with a pulley]—and the blocks all up there, a line, and they'd pull logs out of the swamp. I top-loaded them logs on the cars there until I learnt to handle the loader. Then they took me from that. They put me up on the machine and I loaded the logs. And I done that for a while until I got a little bit higher, then they took me from that and put me to the skidding levers. And I stayed to the levers until—that was the last work I'd done was on the skidders.

See, I just went from one job to another. I reckon I was 'long up in the seventies and eighties on the day when I retired. The last work I done was right back of Conway, down there in them woods—with the fellah they call Graham Holt.

The levers—now like this is the skidder sitting righ' chere. Here is a drum. Here, that's a sort of what you give it the gas with. The one right here is what you press down on to pull your log by. And that was the machine they used to load the log onto the train.

[The tram locomotives] looked like a little [slight chuckle] tumble-along comin' through the woods. They were small and there was some on 'em was pretty good size. They had them named Number Two and Number One and Number Three and Number Four…like that. Number Two was the one that took the logs to the main line—I mean, to the mill. And these others, they'd pull them out of the swamp out to the main line; and then they'd couple up and she'd take them on in to the mill.

Well, I have cut down trees—*big* ol' trees [holds arms up and outward as if embracing something large] like that you couldn't meet around. I have cut them down with an axe. A lot of crosscutting [with a two-man saw]. And I used to cut rider weed [right-of-way (translation by J. Marion Vaught Jr.)]. Like see that swamp there, and cut a road through there. Sometime I'd come into a tree—great, great, big old, big old tree [extends arms horizontally]. And I'd get on my knees and I'd take my axe and I'd cut that tree [close to the ground]. Sometimes it'd take me a day. Sometime I'd cut 'em down less than a day.

I'd climb the trees and hang my rig up the tree [raises arm and pumps upward-facing palm]. Have a belt [rubs right hip]; stick my axe down on there. And I'd go walking up that tree [i.e., with spiked boots] until I wanted to cut the top out, and then I'd start to cuttin' and I'd cut and the top of the lead [hinting at a smile, he leans to left and right quickly to indicate swaying tree]. But I'd know which way it was going to fall to keep it from falling on *me* [laughs].

Mostly I stayed over there. I'd leave here around four o'clock [a.m.]. They had what they called camps. Beside the railroad, a long string of camps. Sometimes there would be two or three stay in a camp; and we'd have what you called old bunk beds in those days. We'd have our fireplace outside and we'd sit on out there and cook our food; and then we'd go inside and eat, fix our bucket and set it up for the next morning.

We'd go to work sometimes six o'clock, sometimes six-thirty. Worked till twelve and knock off and then we'd go back and worked till six.

Lumber maker.

We didn't stop for a rainy day unless'n hit got too bad. Now, if it did, we'd knock off and go back to the camp. We'd always have us a pair of overhalls [overalls], a pair of pants, and a shirt or sumpin' in there. When we'd go on back in wet, we'd pull off our wet clothes and put them on and dry our clothes, then, for the next day. Yes, we worked six days a week. I weren't making nothing then—dollar and a quarter a day long. Yes, ma'am. We had to buy our own food and of course we could take a dollar 'long then and buy what you could buy here now with fifty dollars. You could take ten cents, buy a piece of meat that long [holds hands a foot apart]. Take a dime and you'd buy a quart of rice. The grits—you had no limit to them.

Well, I farmed [pause] later on, I reckon about ten or fifteen years. I'd sell some tobacco in Conway, and I'd sell to Mullins [in Marion County]. And I'd sell some to Fairmont [North Carolina]. I would go wherever I thought I'd get the best price in tobacco. No, ma'am—I was farming for another man, but I was the operator over the farm. I was in charge of the whole farm. It belonged to Elmo Howard. I done the work. He bought the fertilize and he furnished all d' seed. I furnished my own team, and I done the work and me 'n him went half the 'bacca.

No'm, I had one horse [rather than two mules]. I bought the horse from Bob Martin out there at the Allentown. Sometimes I'd ride him [to work], but I didn't like to ride no horse. My farm was all right there at the house [waves hand]. All I had to do was to go out there and catch my horse and go up right there and hook him up [to the plow] and go on to work. I believe I had about six acres of tobacco. Well, I don't know [how much money I made]. This is rightly because I didn't keep no record of that. I made enough money to build this house here and to buy this place and I bought me a truck and I bought me a tractor.

All my life [I've been healthy]. I ain't never been to no doctors. I get to feeling tough, just like I is now. Lay down, take me an Anacin or something or another. Directly, I'd get up and go on, do my work.

Well, now, there was not too much of transportation on the river. The river was just something [leans head in cupped hand] that come from wa-a-y back yonder: *Wacca*maw River, *Pee Dee* River, *Lumber* River, all—all them rivers. Now boats would run up and down this river here, but they would bring fertilize and merchandise for the store; and they would carry back shingles, or lumber, or whatsomever they had, they transferred up and down the river. There wasn't no trucks on the road; and all of the transferring put in there [waves folded paper] was on the river and railroad. And so after later years, they got to inventin' trucks to move the stuff about, but then they—what you might say, they cut the boats out of the river. Nothing didn't run the river now but these little motorboats and fishermen and all like that. Now dey got the river now.

The *Mitchelle C.* and the *Burroughs* was a little larger than the *Ruth* was. The place up there they call Red Bluff, they went that fur. Then they'd turn around; they'd go right back to Conway. Oh, oh, yes, ma'am [I remember the snag boat]. I forgot the name of dat boat now; but hit used to land right down there. They have a place down there they called Old Grahamville [site of a turpentine distillery, later called Wild Horse, located on the other side of Highway 90 from Mr. Vereen's house]. It used to park right down there and then run up and down and clean the river out. It was a *gov'ment* boat. Dey'd come up this river from Conway up into Red Bluff and stay here for *weeks* and *months* and *months* cleaning out the river and cutting the snags and things.

I didn't ride no boat. Now dey had a boat that would go from Conway to Georgetown—the excussion [excursion]. People would go down there, but at that time, I wasn't big enough to get out on no trip.

There ain't no doctor nowhere right close around here. And I 'member Dr. [pauses]—"Dr. Joe" [Joseph Dusenbury], Dr. Norton and I was staying down yonder. I got sick and they come to me and they were driving an old horse and buggy. When people got sick, you'd see one [someone] over there and you could see them with a big old, old hand-light. Then they'd be going to that house where the people were sick at. They'd get herbs out of the woods and make tea, and then they'd go and they'd pray, and they'd sing with them people, and they'd get well. Laura Bellamy was one on 'em, and Charity Grissett. County nurses? They'd give people shots for whatever was wrong with them. If they had measles or chicken pox or other disease that called for a shot.

Right down there [points toward Waccamaw]. When they'd get enough to baptize like five or six, or three or four, they'd go down there and baptize 'em. And they'd come back and they'd receive 'em in the church. The preacher and a group of people would sing, then pray. Well, sometime they would use a hymn [long pause]—let's see now, I wanted to get it right. [By way of suggestion, Catherine sings "By Jordan's stormy bank," but he continues.] I wanted to get it right. I can't think of that hymn now. [Disregards another suggestion, "Shall we gather at the river."] They would sing a song about "Take me to the water. Take me to the water. Let me be baptized." And the other one, I think, was "Meet Me Down at the River of Jordan." [To Catherine's query about full immersion, he raises his head high] Buried under the water. [Oblivious to her next question] Now I remember my song, "'Go preach my gospel,' says the Lord. 'Bid—'" [twenty-minute videotape runs out.]

Well, I went to the ocean a few times. [Smiles] We'd go down there in an old ox and cart. Go right through dese woods here. Yes, sir. I've seen plenty of bears. Bears used to walk right around that road dere every night. I called a game warden and told him I wanted him to come over here. He said, "There *ain't* no *bears* walking up and down the road." I said, "Well you come on." So he come and I said, "Here's the track." And he got to looking [searches the floor in imitation] and he said, "*Gracious God!* These *is* bear tracks, ain't they!"

We'd go 'long on Long Lake in October or November, before it'd get pretty good cold. We'd get the old ox and go right down that road there and go right to the beach. We had what they called a hand seine, and we'd stood on the hill [dune]. We'd catch fish like that—mullets and spots, any kind of fish that would run in the water [migrate southward]. They'd have a big, high barrel [raises arm] and lots of us'd have that barrel jammed full of salt, mullets and spots [to eat during the winter].

I *should* remember the Inland Waterway because I done a lot of work on there. [Pauses, looks steadily at Wells.] When first started the digging, I went for a job, and I'd work for a old man they called Dynamite King. He'd get out in that water up to here [rubs hands across chest], and I'd tote dynamite to 'im, and he'd tell me which way to go to get out of the danger spot. He'd put that dynamite down on it. They had him a lo-ong rod [opens arms to full extension] and he'd crouch down under a stump, so he'd say, "Allrighty buddies, come back thisaway now." And I'd be flotated in that water back there a ways. He had a little wire—I reckon about like this here [points to microphone wire]—and he'd touch them wires together like that, and you'd see that stump go up in the air! [Raises hand.] I worked with him until they got some skidders to pull the stumps and the logs and things off of there. Then I hooked tongs in the woods. I hooked the one skidder and Keeler Sumpter was hooked to the other one, and we cleaned that whole right o' way over here—all the way up.[25]

No, I don't remember the slaves. I heared my old grandmamma talk about the slaves and how dey done people. She'd say that back over the river here [turns to lift arm] is a big old iron-top house setting right 'side the road; and right down from that house was a big old swamp field. And dem people would go up on top of that house [raises arm] where they could watch down in the field [points hand downward] and all them that didn't work like they were supposed to work, when they come out they were tuck up with a whup. I'd ask, "Was you ever whupped?" She said, "No, 'cause I mostly stayed around the house, but I've seen them whip a many of 'em."[26]

Right up there [points up Highway 90 toward the school at the earlier True Vine Church]. Anthony Vaught was one teacher; Olin Chestnut was one, and a girl by the name of Cassie Singletary. And one by the name of Sadie Dewitt. I didn't go to school; I had to work. Sometime I'd go about twenty or thirty days. I larnt a bit of reading and writing, but the mostest that I larned was after I got out from school. I'd set down and take old books and read and try to write. So I learned how to write and I can read right good, but I didn't larn all of that at the school.

[After some persuasion, Wells was able to get Mr. Vereen to climb into the college van, which rattled up Highway 90 to Reaves Ferry and crossed the bridge. As he stood on the bank, the Waccamaw flowed greenly behind him.]

I had a cable across the river with a flat, and I'd pull the cable. [Holds cane parallel to ground and threads it hand over hand.] Pull the flat across. And boat had a paddle. [Shifts cane to his side, pushes it backward.] How old I was—oh, I was nothing but a boy then—fifteen or sixteen years old. There weren't no charge. Just a free ferry. Anybody came and holler they wanted across, whoever was there on, they would put them across. People would be traveling from here going through up the road. They'd know us down on where they'd come across, and some would come over here to buy fertilize. Some would come to buy grocery, all like that. They had a big store sitting right there [on the opposite bank]. We didn't have no troubles or nothing. They just put them across and let them go.

Carrie Daniels Doyle.

Carrie Daniels Doyle

Born 1901

"They really didn't think they could ever live anywheres else."

Richard Gallivant [also spelled Galivant and Gallwant on old maps] would fall out of his boat with astonishment. In the early nineteenth century he operated a ferry across the Little Pee Dee River between Horry and Marion Counties, long before the first bridge appeared in 1902 or 1903 to make one of the few walkable connections between Horry and the mainland of South Carolina. The two-lane version of Highway 501 was built in 1948, and now every day thousands of vehicles rumble across the double bridges—cars, trucks, buses and RVs, often bearing out-of-state license plates, swim gear, golf clubs and souvenir T-shirts.

According to J.William F. "Billy" Holliday, Ph.D. (b. 1942), the highway "plows through and virtually demolishes the beauty and serenity of what Galivants Ferry had been since the 1870s." As it reaches Horry, it passes Pee Dee Farms on the left—a gasoline station, a general store and the headquarters for the Holliday family's operation of tobacco and timberlands, a business that started in the late 1860s. Nearby is a cul-de-sac of several unpainted little houses that have their antitheses in several mansions that are set far back from the highway on the opposite side. Officially called "Holliday Highway" between Galivants Ferry and Conway, Rt. 501 passes the road it replaced, which angles from the beach-bound lanes, runs behind a handsome, four-story red barn, continues through the hamlet and ends nearby at Pee Dee Highway. "Along that dirt road," explains Holliday, "in what was once a lush thicket of pine, gum and oak, a passerby would have seen the heart and soul of Galivants Ferry."

Living there until the late 1950s were a dozen or more families. They all played roles in what was a self-sufficient community: field hands (or day laborers), store and station managers and attendants, a mechanic, farm overseers, maids and yard-men, one general farm manager, a blacksmith in the old days and one bookkeeper in the fifties. Many worked out in the fields, plowed fields with mules (kept in a yard beside the big red barn) or minded the cattle. They rode wagons to and from the fields a half-mile or mile down toward Aynor or south toward Georgetown.

Between 1976 and 1978, Billy crisscrossed Western Horry County to investigate the business practices of his great-grandfather, Joseph William Holliday (1827–1904) or his grandfather, George Judson Holliday (1875–1941).[27] Although Billy's project is ongoing, it already harvested seventeen audiotaped interviews with a dozen people. The sheaf of transcriptions by Karen Hanson, totaling 335 single-spaced pages, was plopped into the hands of the author while he was looking for other material. Most of the transcriptions were eventually corrected by Billy, as well as by the descendants of the people interviewed, then legally released for deposit in Kimbel Library, Coastal Carolina University.[28]

As with most people, Mrs. Doyle's kindly impulses co-exist with less generous biases that reflect her socioeconomic group. White folks in an isolated county were little traveled, light of wallet and more familiar with sweat than ink. As Effie Richardson, a member of the previous generation who had kept house for George J. Holliday at the turn of the century, told Billy: "We didn't know nothing and we didn't have nothing. We just tried to get by." But at least such whites ranked above the Negroes, for whom they often used "the n-word"—a slang term that expressed condescension but not necessarily the mean-spiritedness it would later—instead of the genteel "Nigras" or "colored." Mrs. Doyle's interviews preserve details about the community's people, customs, transportation, day-labor system and commissary system (whereby the company store furnished supplies against future earnings). They also preserve the folk grammar that has been suggested by the author's extra-close re-transcription.[29]

Thirty years after these interviews, Billy generously made corrections and additions to this chapter in several phases.

On September 8, 1976, this friendly reunion conversation took place at Mrs. Doyle's house in Aynor. Carrie spoke with a melodic variety of pitch, prolonged vowels and lavish folk grammar. Browsing through old photographs, the interlocutors discuss people whom Carrie called "Aunt" or "Uncle." One was Tenner Williams.

Yes, Lord, I knowed her. She was more or less kind of a child [under slavery]. And how she was beat! All that we all around the Ferry ever knowed, there was an old house across the road from the church, and old Aunt Tenner lived down there. She raised Rose and Liza and Fanny Lee and Ned. No [she wasn't their mother], they called her "Aunt." She could have been [blood kin]. She worked a lot at Francis's house.[30]

Oh, mercy knows! Billy, that was the meanest thing! She toted her a long cotton limb in her cotton-picking satchel and if she seen them younguns raise up, she'd beat 'em, flail 'em as hard as hard as she could. I have been so sorry for 'em. Poor Rose. Everybody loved Rose Williams, and she'd beat that poor old thing—to *death* just about. [Nobody tried to stop her because] who was daresn to say anything to her? Mr. Coleman'd talk to her sometimes.[31] And that little ol' Fannie Lee was Lizer's child—she come along 'fore Lizer was married. But ol' Aunt Tenner kept Fannie Lee and raised her, and she'd beat the little ol' child to death, just about. Ever she'd walk into a room she'd have a switch stuck in her apron. And when Rose and Walter Williams were goin' together, oh Lord a mercy, she tried to keep Rose shut up. That's right, she knowed how she'd been treated [as a slave] and seemed like she just didn't have no feelings for nobody. She didn't respect nobody. Yes, [in September or October] she would be out in the field! She picked as long as she could. [Chuckles.] She picked cotton 'n hoed cotton, chopped cotton. She was a rough, rough old thing. Right on till she died.

It used to be a habit that people would go off somewheres to a neighbor's house or something, at night and then when they'd start home they would sing the holler. And you could hear 'em, my mercy....Well, you know, some people can whistle and some can't. It was just a custom. Whenever the day's work was done and they'd go to hollerin' at the cotton. [Pause.] People don't live now like they did then. They was a lot of fun people. Lord a mercy, I think back and that Ferry used to be a lively place—they really didn't think they could ever live anywheres else, 'n all of 'em's dead 'n gone, most of 'em. It was home to 'em.

Oh, yes, Mr. Coleman was liked. He worked for George just like he did for Francis. There used to be a old blacksmith shop there, and people'd have de horses and mules shoed and a lot of plows fixed. Mr. [name withheld], he run that old blacksmith shop till he died. He lived till he died right there in the front of the lot of that old house. [She names the four or five children.] He was as big a drunk as there ever was.

Francis and Mr. Coleman would open that commissary on Wednesday night and Saturday evening, and when they knowed that all of 'em got their groceries they would close it. Each one of them would have what they called "cash books." [Billy shows her a book of coupons that could be exchanged for merchandise.] This is one of Mr. George's books. You could go in there 'n buy cloth, anything with those books, and the bookkeeper would know how many days they had worked and all and what they got. Sometimes they would get worried and aggravated, they didn't think they ought to know, and they'd ask for a bigger book. This was a dollar book, so you see they got twenty-seven dollars.

Yes, Lord, I remember the commissary at Francis's! [Laughs.] See, Francis just had groceries; Mr. George had material—most anything. The Ferry store has been there since Mr. Joe Holliday, but I don't remember him. It used to be just a long, plank, wooden building with wooden counters. People who lived on a farm owned by George used his store, and the same with Francis.[32] [She names a half-dozen farms, one owned by the prosperous Jess Gray Parker, whose similar appearance to Jesse Holliday, first son of Joseph and his first wife, evokes some mirth.] He didn't have nothin' to leave him, Jesse Holliday didn't. He [Jesse] worked there for his mother [Flora Holliday, George's wife] for a long, long time. I patched his clothes and fixed 'em. [Laughter and more discussion of the Jesses.]

They didn't go get the tobacco gatherers then like they do now for everybody around—that theecket [thicket] was full o' little houses and somebody lived in every one of them, and each one would swap work. My brother, he farmed there. Well, Mr. Coleman would always see that each farmer had help to gather the tobacco. [She names people who lived in the community.] Ol' Miz Martha Smith lived there and her girls worked for George Holliday at his house; one was a nurse and one cooked. Yeah, they was white.

There was about equal [half the people white, half black], I reckon. They worked together 'n got along good. But niggers, they knowed they's niggers then. And they put themselves in their place—not like it is now.[33]

Old Aunt Tenner? She was well thought of and well respected because she was old, a slave—slavery. Old Uncle Horace and Aunt Polly, they weren't slavery. Lizer named Tenner Riggins [who died in 2007 at the age of 84] after her. [Billy expresses amazement.] Oh, yes, Lord, they did love Auntie!

I remember whenever Miss Nettie died [second wife of J.W. Holliday]. [Looking through the photographs] I remember one Christmas, Miss Nettie was sick—she died of TB. [Her voice becomes barely audible. She describes the house.] They drove to the cemetery in a horse and carriage. It was a big, long thing with tassels hanging all around the inside. Hit come from Marion, and they called it the hearse carriage. Yeah, it had glass around it and curtains hanging on the inside with big balls. I was little, but I remember whenever they come marching out and all the rest were in buggies, too. Miss Nettie, before she died, she had a buggy horse and the horse was named Little Bit. And Francis used that horse and Mr. Coleman used it. A mad dog bit that horse and it went mad. They had to shut her in the stable. I don't remember whether she finally died or they killed her. They hated it so bad—but the horse just reared and knocked that stable.

No, no. George didn't go out into the field! [Laughs.] He stayed in that office—all de time. Unless he was in the Keeley [drying-out].[34] [They discuss his alcoholism, for which he was treated most often in Greensboro, North Carolina.] In the commissary sometimes it would be pleasant and sometimes unpleasant. And he'd tell his secretary what to do 'n how to do 'n who to let have 'n who to not let have. They'd come out a rarin' 'n a quarrelin', mad with her and she'd have to do as she was told. She'd be the one to give them the coupon book. He would tell her how much to let 'em have. He done good by 'em. [Indignant] You can't hand out everything in the world that you got. Oh, yes [people came from all over], all around Jordansville and all. There was no place else they knowed that they could go and live. Yes, my mercy, everybody knowed it! "Well, we've got to live somewheres and this is the best place." There weren't no jobs [in town] or nothing like there is now. Yes. Eat and work.

And when 'bacca getherin' time come, Mr. Coleman'd go around and see he had one to gether one day and 'nother to gether another day. Hit was a big, big place.

[They discuss the possibility that Will Marlowe was the son of Joseph W. Holliday.] "Well, it could have been true. Mr. George gave Will a home for as long as he lived, and Will Marlowe was Mr. George Holliday's right-hand man. Yes, hauling stuff from Georgetown he worked on that old flat [a raft-like boat with a flat bottom and square ends that remains under water at Galivants Ferry]. After they parked it there hit just stayed in the water and rotted away. It was just a long, flat thing; it had some logs around the edges. Every Christmas the people around there'd order whiskey for Christmas and it'd come in on that flat. My daddy would. They'd get glass jugs—a bunch of them'd go two or three together and get a gallon—well, one of them glass jugs would hold about a gallon. But you didn't hear much of it except at Christmas. Some would make grape juice—you know in grape time—and make grape wine. Oh, no, no [there weren't any liquor stores]. [Some would make their own whiskey] and call it cornbuck, and they'd make grape wine. People used to make a lot of syrup out of sugar cane—well, they would take that cane skin [the bagasse] and make some kinda ol' drink of hit.

Yes [I've seen remnants of the turpentine industry]. People used to make soap and I've been there many a time to dig rawzin [rosin] to make soap. There used to be a rawzin still there, but I don't remember that. It was across the road next to the river. People'd would dig down and get pretty, clear hunks to put in their soap. They'd take lye and meat skins and old grease, Red Devil lye and that rawzin to make it smell good and fresh. People would save old meat skin and old grease. They called it the lye soap, that's what people washed with. Every family there'd make it. If they made it till the full of the moon, the soap would shrink up. They'd make it of th'evening and leave it set in the pot all night and then the next morning get out there and cut it up in pieces and lay it about to dry. They did that till [manufacturers] went to making boxes and powders.

They made it 'n sold it. I heard the older people talkin' about it. They would put the rawzin [likely all the turpentine distillates] in barrels and then pole it down the river. I would hear Will Marlowe's wife talking; he would be gone about a week sometimes. They would all gether down there whenever the flat came back.[35] Yes, they also went down to the river to water the cattle with. They would have to haul a lot of times. Francis had a lot—he had pastures. That big pecan field across to John Monroe's was one. [John Monroe Holliday was Billy's uncle.] [Vigorously] They used to keep that riverbank just as slick as glass a-settin' on it a-fishin'. There'd be a lot o' people that, if they'd see somebody at a certain place, they would have them get away and say, "That was our fishing place." Yes, you could heah anybody all over de place out a-callin' their children or talkin' to 'em.

A lot of people duck hunt. A lotta people took two automobile wheels 'n made a cart. They called 'em the Hoover carts.[36] Well, it just had one seat and I mean it'd bounce you. A mule'd pull 'em. All them mules was named, too. Ol' Miz [name withheld] had three boys; them was the meanest things to mules. The other men had their teams and they wouldn't let the [name withheld] boys work 'em. They'd beat them mules to death and make 'em run, trot, I mean with loads.

Just to get to thinkin' back to times like that…Most of 'em's all dead and—niggers 'n white. Now everything I've told you is the truth.

October 31, 1976

This interview was conducted on a motor tour of the Galivants Ferry area. Billy, half her age, directs the conversation in an intense staccato, but at times Carrie becomes his docent. Usually serene, she does get worked up about various subjects and even returns a few of Billy's interruptions. At times, the interview suggests a duet between soprano and tenor about yesteryear. It begins in that part of the community called Bayfield, across Highway 501 from Pee Dee Farms headquarters. (A bay is a low area, often a Carolina Bay, thick of foliage.) After spying the old packhouse, where cured tobacco was stored, she looks at the dwellings.

And that was a little old longhouse, with one partition through it and one bedroom in the back and then a big ol' clay chimley in the front. On the end was just a little ol' shed like for the kitchen. They used a lot of light from the fireplace [for illumination]. They didn't have no lamps. Some people did [have kerosene lamps], and some of 'em didn't have a chimney on it—just a little old smoking flame.[37] Yes, they'd smoke. That's what they was used to. [Sound of a vehicle zooming past. They drive across Highway 501 and continue the session behind the general store with Carrie exclaiming in a sweet, delighted tone] Well there's the 'tater house; it's still there. Oh, yes, I remember when hit was built. There is the old blacksmith shop.[38] And that's the old [gasoline] station. And there is the [grist] mill house, after the big 'un burned down, then they built that one. And they run this mill house by a tractor. Hit was a big old mill grinding and gin house for cotton and then they had a machinery that would grind corn and meal and grits. The day that hit burnt down Dora Marlowe said that Mr. George Holliday didn't miss that like she would her old homemade eatin' table [if it had burned up]. [Laughs.] She done her biscuits on that table. Well, she meant that she wouldn't have nothin' to fall back on. One Sat'dy it burnt down.

[Billy drives back across the highway to Bayfield, where the discussion of houses resumes behind the barn.] One, two, three four—I know there used to be four back there. I wouldn't o' never knowed this place. It used to be full of pines and just as clean…When Mr. George or your daddy or any of 'em would have lumber, they'd pile it good 'n straight out there. Whenever they was buildin' this—it was always called the New Building. Oh, my mercy. Look out there at the trees—hit's growed up. Now this old sweet gum tree was there. Yeah, [the barn was painted] bright red. But… your daddy [J.W. Holliday, 1912–1981] and them went to painting the houses and covering them and putting bathrooms in them and remodeling them. Yeah, the houses had wood shingles. Oh, my Lord. Will Smith lived there for years and years. Years ago Monroe Richardson lived there. [On Monday morning] everyone would get up and meet at the lot. His job would be driving the wagon. They didn't have no trucks then. He would haul fertilizer and things like that, corn, cotton. [They greet Clyde Register in another vehicle.]

No, Mr. Press Coleman was in charge. Start about sunrise—they'd all go there and get the teams. Oh, my mercy, that lot would be full—the mules, my mercy, 'n each one had their team, Mr. Wiggins and Monroe, Gurley Graham, a lot of the others, too. Yeah, they'd eat breakfast 'fore that. This whole place was farmed then with mules. And in the summertime they'd plow—from sunup to sundown. Yes, it was hard. Ooh, you just don't know. No, they wouldn't [talk about the hardships].

In the spring of the year whenever it come time to haul fertilizer, they had to go to Rains [in Marion County] or t' Aynor 'cause it come in on the train. In the summer they'd plow the corn and sow the peas. Pull the fodder 'n break the corn. Way 'long then [in the 1920s] there weren't much tobacca, but they'd have big cotton crops [grown until the late 1950s]. Yes [they'd pick cotton this time of year], cotton 'n dried peas. Nothin' [would be in the wagons when they went out into the fields at about 7:30 a.m.] Whenever they'd go with the plows—well now, then, they'd unhook the mules from the plows 'n leave the plows in the field, 'n maybe they'd ride the mules onto the lot [bareback]. Whenever they would go to break the corn [pull the ripe ears off the stalk] 'n leave it in little piles, then they would take the two-horse wagon and go out there and load up them wagons with corn. Or cotton, hay and fodder. The one that fed the animals, he would put everyone's team, corn and hay and stuff, in the stables.

Walkin'! A lot of times the cotton pickers would ride back on the wagons, but they went out there walking.

I reckon he'd [Monroe Richardson] be breakin' corn. They would do that hollering mostly late of the evenings. Not in the morning. Sometimes I hear a record that reminds me of it so much [Eddie Arnold's "Cattle Call" (1961–1962).] 'Course then people didn't know what radio or television or talking machine or nothing was. Yeah, kind of like a yodel. No [not everybody could do it]! It was lonesome and would sound way off. Lot of times I could be at home in the yard, or in the field. You could hear the wagons coming while you were picking cotton, and be so glad, we'd gather the cotton and tie up our sheet. Monroe 'n Walter Williams, they was the main wagons. Whether it was at the end of the row or not, we'd 'preciate it. Oh, yes [we'd talk while picking cotton]. Sometimes we'd have a good time. Then again, we'd get tired…'n they'd get fussin'…Well, they'd be about haif 'n haif [blacks and whites].

Oh, mercy, yes. [I've been in the old barn] hundreds of times. They built a driveway up there and them trucks'd haul tobacco up there—there were some trucks then. Yes, I tied tobacco—on the second floor.

[Off they drive.] Tenner's old house used to be back there. Yes, that's hers, one of them little old 'uns—still there. Little old room off the po'ch [porch]—that was the kitchen. This was the wagon shed right here where they kept all of the wagons and things. Over yonder where that yellow thing is, that was the corn shed, where they put the corn 'n the hay and feed 'n stuff, and right acrost in front of it was the mule stables.

That's where your grandmother and your granddaddy lived, and all their children was born there. We called it the Holliday House. [We called Francis's house—across the highway—Miss Nettie's House.] Yes, this is where my daddy lived for years 'n years, 'n died there. They remodeled this house—your mother had that done herself. And back over there was Miss Flora's washhouse. Ooh, these ditch banks was always cleaned off just as clean! You cain't now for trees. [More talk about houses in the old days.] That highway wasn't there when they remodeled it. This here was the only road. There used to be a house we called the Dell House, where Miss Nettie Holliday's cook lived, Dell Marlowe [sister of Will]. She had her mother and her sister, Rutilda.

This here [a grove of pecan trees] used to be a forty-acre cotton patch. And on the left, too, cotton. This place up here [on Pee Dee Road] was called the Windy Hill. Walter Williams lived in this house. [Yes, he was a black man and one of the people who hollered. Yes, you could tell the difference between people's styles] just like you can by one a-talking. [name withheld] lived here—hit was an old, cold open house, and she took [name withheld] there 'n she raised him in that house. I know when we went there to see him she had him by the fireplace and him all wropped up and she a-crying and scared he was going to die. He was so little and puny, 'n his mama dyin'. And a lot of people'd 've been better off it he had o' died. [They laugh. When Billy asks why, she adds that he mainly hurt himself rather than others, then changes the subject.]

[For another hour they continue driving, road by field, house by name, farm by story, farm bell by turpentine pot.] There used to be a big swamp here, and they called it Over the Bay, and there was foot-logs that you had to walk. This used to be called Scarborough Branch. Wagons could come through, it was walking that was hard, those bogs. And people had those planks to walk on.

[They pass the house of Burt Parker, who got rich by working; the old Red-Top House; the office of Dr. Truluck, who burned out Carrie's tonsils; the former commissary; the old Confederate woman's house—she was old slavery; the house Billy lived in as a child; a graveyard with stones dating back to 1840, burial place of Mr. Coleman. Carrie explains that people swept yards with galberry branches, houses with broom straw; and she recalls that Nellie Moore was a colored widow who lived with her daughter.]

Your grandmother, Miss Flora, she couldn't never learn to drive a car good. They called this the private road from here up to the house, and she went down here 'n got some lumber 'n was carryin' it back 'n had a wreck right there, just run into something 'n the lumber went through the windshield. [They laugh.]

[Noise of their car and the old audiotape begin to resemble a heavy rain. The original transcriber adds: "Billy, there is a pretty long part in there that I can't hear a damn word either of you are saying."] This road was a pure sand bed. People got about with a mule and wagon; they didn't have horses. I remember when Mr. George—they had a surrey they would bring to church. No one else. Mr. Charlie Gerald had kinda big long buggy and Mr. Jesse Price had one and Mr. Coleman he drove a horse and buggy. Most of the time they would just walk. [Talk about churchgoing almost inaudible.] And then on Saturday and Sunday [the women] would get together, bunches of them, and just go off walking over the river bridge. There'd be married women, young girls.

[Billy asks again about the kerosene lamps.] They just couldn't afford them or didn't think about them, and whenever they would go to eat they would have. They would hold it in one hand and eat with the other. Now that is the truth. I don't know how they did it.

Rilla Cook McCrackin.

Rilla Cook McCrackin

Born 1939

"We slept outside under the roof of the barn's shelter and on top of the tobacco bench."

This chapter owes its existence to the Southern Cluster, an interdisciplinary program once sponsored by the Edwards College of Humanities and Fine Arts at Coastal Carolina University. In 2002, the author took advantage of its brief existence by modifying English 459, Advanced Composition and Rhetoric, just enough to make it one of the eight courses on Southern themes.

One of the students, Amanda McCrackin, youngest of twelve children, interviewed her mother at 3465 Highway 308, Rehobeth Section, then did a transcription. Rilla is herself the youngest person included in this book (born thirty-eight years after Carrie Doyle). The wife of Sam T. McCrackin, she is the daughter of James Walter Cook (b. 1912) and Pincey Cook (b. 1921), who had died two weeks earlier. Her grandmother, Maggie Johnson, helped plant the oak trees that line the streets of Aynor.

A year or so after the interview, the author paid a visit to the McCrackins' acreage, which somehow rose above the swamps and creeks some miles east of Galivants Ferry. To him, the Confederate flag seemed to cast a bigger shadow than the American flag above it on the tall pole, but he soon became fond of Rilla and S.T., who welcomed him warmly and even gave him a show-and-tell inventory of old-time tools stored in outbuildings.

Rilla has an eye for details—technical, social, sensory and emotional—that a novelist might envy, especially on the subject of tobacco, Horry's main cash crop after the turn of the twentieth century. She augmented the transcription several times, both within the text and on appended sheets; the latter additions appear in parentheses. This is the only transcription that the author did not review against the tape.

The author also held interviews with another former sharecropper, Claudia A. Brown (b. 1901), who was introduced to him by Woodrow Long.

I can remember when I was four years old. I was walking on a dirt road with my mama, holding her hand and a stick of dog fennel in my other hand jabbing in the dirt. The sun was bright. I had on a white dress Ma made for me out of bleached rice sacks; she sewed it by hand. All my clothes were made by Mama until I got out of grammar school; some were made out of hog feed sack. That's when we stayed on the Holliday farms at Galivants Ferry, called the Bayfield. I can remember riding on the mule and wagon between my mama and daddy going through a swamp and going to the river fishing.

I can tell how hard it was to make a living back then. My daddy having to plow with an ol' mule and having to cut hedgerow with bush axes in the wintertime. Couldn't do it in the summer time 'cause it was too hot. You could get cool drinks of water from creeks back then without worry of poison. I could remember trying to help stacking limbs. We traded work with other farmers. From time I was a little girl till the time I was grown, we farmed. In the fall of 1947 we moved to Fort Mill, South Carolina, to work in Springs Cotton Mill so we would have enough money to survive through until spring. We always would come back to the country to start again. We farmed corn cotton and 'bacco. We grew sweet 'taters for ourselves and neighbors and friends; we would grow a garden every year and Mama always canned vegetables in summer.

Come time to take the tobacco out to the flue-cured barns, we had a 'bacco drag lined with fertilizer sacks (burlap, guano) that had been washed, opened up, and sewn together by hand with tobacco twine and placed on the inside of a drag to hold it in place. It was called the flat drag. [About three feet high at the top], the drag is six, seven, eight feet long, lined on the inside from top to bottom with guano sacks, then tacked down. It has two-by-eights for sides. It lasted all season through and the tobacco was carried to the barn from the field by the mule the latter part of June. When the tobacco was green, we cropped off the stalks and placed it in the tobacco drag by hand. The drag was pulled by a mule and the tobacco was put in it. There was no fifth middle [an unplanted row for a tractor to drive between two sets of double rows] back then. At poisoning time, a drag with a sprayer attached had to be pulled down rows with a barrel with poison pulled by the mule. Sometimes we had to go down rows in early spring. We had to go down rows and put poison in the bud of plants with our hands to kill the budworms when it was a foot or two high.

The beds were tilled and made ready to sow in mid January. Green reeds were cut in one-foot lengths across, enough to stake canvases down over the beds along each side and at the ends of the beds. (The beds ranged in width and length a few inches either way but came out eight feet wide and one hundred feet long.). You had to pull the plants from the 'baccer beds before they could be planted. Everybody's back hurt. You would be tired and cold in the dew of the morning. Your fingers ached, your back ached and your knees were wet and cold. You were glad when the sun warmed things up in the morning.

When the tobacco was being planted (set out), women were carrying pasteboard boxes with holes in each end tied with string and put a piece of cloth around their necks that came down to the waist. The plants were put in a box and put in a hand-setter by the ladies. They had to face the men and walk back'ards to drop the plants in the setter. The men carried hand-setters—with a place for water. It had a handle, and under the handle was a place where the water went—a trough. The men would walk.

When I was a little girl I had to tote buckets of water down to the field. I was about six years old; my bucket was made from a three-pound coffee can with wire bales. I always got my dress wet. (Girls didn't wear pants much back then.) The water was taken from a barrel and carried to put in setters. Having to pull the plants from the 'baccer beds was an awful job. Everybody's back hurt from squatting and reaching across the beds. The plants were packed in tobacco drags in rows and carried to the field.

I remember getting up with no electricity. Going to school. Before daddy could get the fire in the fireplace made, Mama would have me dressed. I would not eat breakfast. I had to walk to school about two miles to Mill Swamp School in Galivants Ferry. I went also to Rehobeth School in the Rehobeth Section on what is now Nichols Highway. I walked through a wet swamp on old, hollow cypress logs left by loggers many years before. My daddy walked me across the swamp and talked to me as I went through

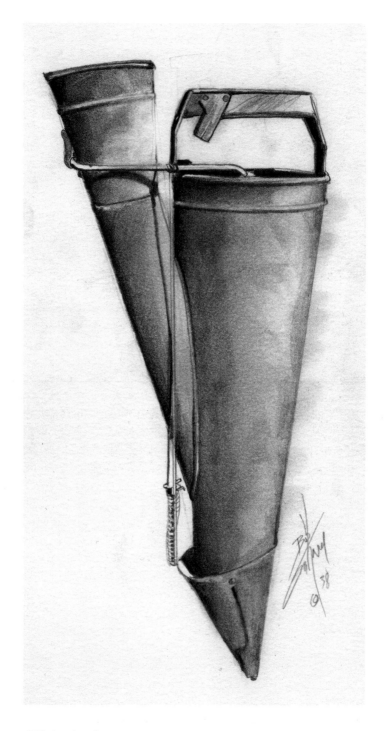

Old-time hand-setter.

the woods out to the old field where the road to the school was. Daddy sometimes—if the water got too high—he took me on the mule's back and came to pick me up that afternoon.

Then later, Aynor High School, I walked every morning and walked back home every afternoon. There was no lunchroom and I took a biscuit with a piece of fatback or either a fried egg in it. Sometimes I had peanut butter and Saltine crackers for lunch. There was a little store close to Mill Swamp School; Mr. Bernice Vaught owned it. Sometime I would get me a orange drink (Nehi) or six-ounce Coke for lunch if Daddy would have six cents. There was no highways from Aynor back to there. All dirt roads. We use to shop at Cool Spring store to get meal, flour, rice, sugar. It was bought in the bulk.

I remember going with my mom and dad to the street dance in Aynor; it was not called the Hoedown then. We went on a mule and wagon. People danced, played music with their own instruments, sometimes till 12:30 or 1:00 a.m. We went to the movies often, too. There was a theater [that] had an upstairs where the black people could go see the movie; tickets were sold separately at that time.

[As a child] I was real sickly. I had a low blood count and stayed on vitamins and tonics. These were bought from Watkins 'n Raleigh peddlers out of their cars.[39] Blood transfusions, blood and liver shots. That went on until I was eighteen. I had pneumonia, tonsillitis, the flu, measles when I was a child. I had the toothache a lot. My daddy managed to go to the doctor and get medicine.

We didn't have electricity so we had to use the wood stove in the kitchen for heating and cooking, or the fireplace in the living room. We had board floors with open cracks in them; wind blew in, winter and summer. We had an old toilet outside. When I was eleven, electricity finally come through to our house. We only had lights, no running water. Still no bathroom. We had to pump the water. Every few years we would move to another location. The winters didn't get any warmer and the summers didn't get any cooler. I was eighteen before we got a bathroom and it was not in the house. The water would freeze in the commode at night. It was in a hulled-up room on the back porch. We never had a hot water heater until I was married with children. Three children anyway.

We had a big pile of stove wood cut in the fall after the crop was finished. It was put with easy access to the kitchen but the well or pump was still outside day or night. You would have to prime the pump or draw water from the well to cook, bathe or wash clothes in the wash-pot and scrub-board.

(Some of the farms my daddy sharecropped had very sandy land. It wasn't hard to disk or plow. It seemed like a fine grade of sand, not dark or coarse, and Daddy always seemed to do well with it.) Sometime some of the crop would be lost to too much water caused by gales. Sometime it would not make well (the water level would not be high enough to pump) because of the drought. Just like now it is a risk everyone must take. We raised hogs, chickens, cows, and had plenty of garden when the weather was good. I think we were sorta like the crops; if the weather wasn't good for the crops it wasn't good for us either. But having family and friends through the good and the hard times made life bearable.

(Some landowners had small buildings that the black people stayed in. No running water or bathrooms. Some had a small wood stove to cook on. Hand-wash their clothes and hang them on a fence or limbs of trees. They did not go into white people's houses. I think people were afraid of them because of their color and few had any education. They didn't have very much to say. They worked hard for what they got. Some would have to hitchhike back to their home if they failed to work or couldn't handle the heat. Some were middle-age women with their children that were old enough to work in tobacco.)

(Yes, it was hard. The summers were suffocating. There was no ice water—barn or field—just a gallon jug taken to the field. The menfolk cropping tobacco would drink from the branch in the woods if the water was running and clear. Daddy said it was all right to drink unless you saw a dead varmint close by.)

(The bench is where the tobacco was placed from the drag that brought the green tobacco from the field to the barn. Someone was always available to take it out of the drag and place it on the tobacco bench with stems toward handers and stringers. The handers picked it up three or four leaves at the time, keeping stems level to be strung by the stringer. Just anyone wasn't chosen to string tobacco; it had to be done a certain way—neatly 'n tight so as not to fall out of the thread wrapped around it because the tobacco was being heated, and gradually the stems of tobacco would shrink and could fall out of the wrapped strings.)

(Children could hand tobacco and women strung it on the stick by wrapping thread around the bat of tobacco—a "bat," three or four leaves at one time—then gripping it and sliding it up tight to the stick. The next bat would be wrapped with the string the same way and thrown over the stick, and this was a continuance to the end of the stick. The twine would be bound to the end of the stick with about five inches left to hang on the tier poles made from young pine trees with their bark skinned off. The sticks were hung in a staggered position so the heat could circulate better. The poles ran between the front and back of the barn, four feet apart, and rose high to the roof in parallel ranks, maybe seven or eight poles high. A worker or two would have to straddle the poles and scramble around like a circus performer. Sweat and water dripped down to the dirt floor.)

Family and friends helped to cut trees to put into the furnace of the barns. (The flues were made of tin about one foot in diameter. They reached around the barn inside on the sand equally apart carrying heat from fire in the brick furnaces outside the barn, where it was stoked night and day as needed to carefully monitor the heat. The tobacco also has a better aroma when cured well.) Mama and me had to stay there and watch the tobacco while Daddy was running up on the tobacco, raising the heat gradually—that's when the color begins to set in the tobacco leaf and has to have the right amount of heat at the right time or it will come out sorta green and not yellow or too brown; or too much heat would cause the life in the tobacco to be dried out and you could not get anything for it. It would be called "trash," a cheaper grade. Later, farmers progressed enough that they were able to get kerosene to cure tobacco with for heat.

Curing was memorable because I was with my mama and daddy. We slept outside under the roof of the barn's shelter and on top of the tobacco bench. My daddy and mama made us a bed by folding a homemade quilt for each of us on the bench. The mosquitoes were terrible, so to keep them out, Daddy would take an old tobacco canvas to hang up around us as we lay on the bench on a quilt. The mosquitoes whined all night.

After the tobacco was cured, the barn doors would be left open all night for the night air to soften the tobacco. It was called "ordering the tobacco up." The leaves would become more pliable and soft—easy to work with, not break or shatter. Sometime the nights would be very dry and the next morning the tobacco would shatter; you had to be very careful with it.

The cured tobacco was taken out of the barn and packed into the drag lengthwise before dawn. Men climbed up on the tier-poles and handed the tobacco down to the man below him. The lantern was used to break the dark inside the barn and outside. After reaching the top of the drag, the sticks of tobacco were turned crosswise and laid from the front to the back of the drag as high as it could be reached.

It was taken to our house because at that time we had no packinghouse on the farm Daddy sharecropped. Our beds were moved out on the front porch usually first of July and the tobacco was piled up to the ceiling on both sides of the bedroom. A piece of cloth was put over the window so the sun wouldn't bleach the color from the tobacco; our quilts were thrown over it

Squirrel with "wolves."

to keep the moisture in the tobacco. It was taken out of the barn as early as possible before the sun came up. We always carried the flashlight or lantern to break the darkness inside the barn, and the men always came out washed down in sweat. When tobacco was taken to the house at night, we slept outside on the porch. A tobacco canvas was tacked up all around the beds and overhead to keep out some of the mosquitoes. We had company often. Company slept on the porch with a folded quilt called a pallet.

After curing the tobacco, there was taking off tobacco. This is dried tobacco, unstrung and then graded into three grades. First grade, second grade and trash. The next step was to gather a handful, with level stems. Folding a soft leaf you would carefully wrap it around the top part of the leaves and push the stem through the leaves to hold in place. Then later it would all be placed in sticks again and packed down in a neat pile to later take to the warehouse.

On the weekends there were git-togethers. People grew peanuts and would have peanut-poppins. They would also have chicken bog [a Lowcountry pilau made of chicken, sausage, onion and rice] and invite people over to work in the tobacco. The men would all get together and saw wood to fuel the barn's furnaces and for wood stoves (cook stoves and fireplaces). At the house they would be in the yard, the children playing, them having their mandolins, guitars. There was harmonicas sometimes. Some would have a fiddle. Sometimes they would be a-dancin' and some drinkin' stumphole (moonshine, which was still being made and peddled in the fifties). Homemade grape wine was also made and brought for the git-togethers. The little kids playing chase and hide 'n go seek. Children didn't have to have a flashlight back then; their eyes adjusted to the night light—moon and stars. We had lots of fun playing outside at night.

Back those days you would share work. Sharecroppers to me meant you would help one another work. The landowners were the one you had to share the money with—which wasn't hardly enough to pay the debts after the landlord got his portion and Daddy paid his bills for supplies and equipment parts. We had to buy grocery on a credit every year and all things we needed to make the crop with.

Daddy would gear the mule up to the wagon with fishin' poles and dig some bait, enough for me and Mama. Maybe a bat of hay for the mule and maybe a few ears of corn, a few tow sacks, and a quilt and head to the Little Pee Dee River. We would head to Sandy Island, or the Joe Patch, or the Ferry. We would go to Canoe Lake and Nancy's Island. Sometimes he took the one-man boat and sometime not. If the water was high we couldn't camp. Me and Mama could fish on the hills and wade in the sloughs; that is where I learned to paddle a boat. Daddy was afraid I would get drownded.

We would go prepared to spend the night. We would cook and eat 'em and go gather some moss out of the trees. We would pile it under the wagon. Daddy would take the bits out of the mules' mouth and hitch 'em to a tree. He would put the tow sacks on the moss under the wagon and put the quilt on that with an ol' spread on top of us. Sometimes I would think about the snakes that might be crawlin' out there. I would listen to the mule stompin' his feet. Daddy would rake a clean spot on the white sand and pile some leaves on it and light it to run the mosquitoes off. We'd listen to the mosquitoes whine around us at night and Daddy would keep the fire going and fix it to make smoke. That was the good old days.

(Sometimes Daddy would leave the field while plowing and un-gear the mule, water him and put him in the stall. Then he'd dig some bait worms, gather his poles and tackles, and off to the Little Pee Dee River he'd go, walking. When he'd return just before dark he would have a string of fish—a limb cut just below its forked branch and the fish laced onto the longest branch through their gill. My mother would clean the fish and ready the wood stove. We had company often that loved fish. Lots of people talked about Daddy being such a good fisherman. He would say, "You need not even fish if the turtles are on the logs; the fish won't bite."

In later years loggers went into Gunters Island [a large, isolated, low area adjoining the river] and really made a mess of the woods and wagon trails; you could hardly get to the river. When the river was high, Daddy would fish in a treetop that had fallen into the river, possibly from a storm. The line would be as long as his pole and he had a ball of bait bigger than a bum marble—about one inch in diameter—on his hook. He didn't ever seem to have a problem coming out of the treetops without some flatfish—morgans or catfish. The catfish could be skinned and fried, or made into huge pot of catfish stew. This was made by sautéing four or five large onions in a little bit of lard or fried meat grease, then laying the catfish pieces that had been cut up after dressing them on top of the onion, then when color of meat turns white, turn meat over, add salt and pepper and one portion of water—suitable for amount of fish—cover and cook about twenty-five to thirty minutes on medium heat. Add ketchup to your taste and stir gently. Cook on low for a few minutes. Serve with rice or Saltine crackers.)

We ate hash coon and squirrels in the winter. In the spring he would kill rabbits. Some years there would be wolves [weevils] in the squirrels and we couldn't eat them. These were black, fuzzy worms that were hatched from an egg laid by a fly of some kind. They would bore themselves in to the squirrel's body and eat and grow, making the squirrel sick. If cold weather didn't come and kill the wolves, the squirrel would get sick 'n die.[40]

What else can I say? My daddy was a great farmer and fisher; he provided for us well and he was a lovin' father. My mama was a hard workin' woman and she took care of me through sick times. She and my daddy had taken care of her remaining family because her daddy had died. They got married when she was fifteen years old and she finished raising her brother and sisters helpin' out her mama, so I grew up with all of them being like my brothers and sisters. It never took my daddy away from me but he took care of them until they were married. That was in hard times, a lot harder than when I was little. I am their only child.

I love Horry County and I love that it is a part of my life. I was born here and I hope I die here.

Gary M. Mincey and Douglas B. Bailey.

Gary M. Mincey
&
Douglas B. Bailey

Born 1907 and 1907

"[The Good Lord's] never furnished me no wealth, but I've had ideal friends."—Gary Mincey.

The leaves on the two old pecan trees shoosh, bob and thrash as the edge of a rusty metal roof lifts and falls back with a clatter onto a two-story barn. It had once served as a packhouse for tobacco, and porches used to extend above and below so that farmers could grade the cured leaves outside in the cooler air. Other roofs, also rusty-orange, cover tobacco-curing barns, unpainted and obsolete. Despite the windy drama, the air is bright and warm as three longtime friends, smiling, climb the porch steps into the barn, where they tour the first floor with its archaic tools.

It is 1990 and Gary Mincey and Douglas Bailey have just enjoyed a reunion-interview with Catherine Lewis at 4380 Pickney Road, Floyds Township. A double-wide mobile home has replaced the old farmhouse built by Gary's parents, Russ (1881–1967) and Carrie (1887–1973). Ten years earlier the house was a casualty of fire, the same phenomenon that had also destroyed the originals of two Holliday mansions in 1943 and 1977. Both Gary and Doug Bailey wore shirtsleeves, and from Doug's pocket stuck a pen and a note card. Mincey resembled a summer Santa Claus without the beard.

Comfortable in his recliner, he laughed often and spoke in a brogue that may no longer exist, often pronouncing "the" as "dee." Doug, slight of build and gentle of demeanor, smiled with his arms usually folded and talked rapidly. As the air conditioner whirred, an appreciative Catherine sat on the couch next to Doug, who as a young man had lived with her family, the Henifords, for nine years and was like a brother to her.

The author thanks Carrie Angel Mincey Bruno (b. 1977) for sharing a written portrait of her grandfather. She notes that before becoming a game warden, Gary had worked as a farmer, soldier, truck driver, land surveyor, carpenter, steel worker and operator of a cold-storage outfit/general store; he had also helped build a dam for the TVA [Tennessee Valley Authority]. See also Catherine's interview with Doug's wife, Annie Lee Singleton Bailey, a former mail carrier (1993).

Mincey: It come natural [to hunt and fish]. I can remember how bad I'd hate to get up of a morning and my father would say, "Now, if we can catch up with dee work, we'll go fishing at the end of the week." They just loved to hunt and fish. And back at that time, we had much game in this area—and fish—it was unbelievable about the fish we had. The small fish would come right up by de ditch out here from the mill pond [points toward Grainger Mill Pond a mile away and half a mile long].

Bailey: I remember when they used to grind cane over there across Grainger. Made syrup.

Mincey: Around 1915 they burnt a tarkle [tar kiln] right over here where they got the lightwood [dead pinewood saturated with flammable resin] off'n the mill pond [prolonging the vowels of the last two words]. It's elevated slightly—they covered the wood [his hands form a mound]. As the fire burnt, it backs that out. They got trowels, and at the back end of the tarkle they got a place for the barrel, for the tar.

Another thing's a lost art is de boat-makin'. Well, they'd take these logs, big nice cypr'ss. Back then they had ideal trees for that. They'd split a log about the length they wanted the boat, and then they began to hew it out and they shaped the outside of the boat. [He illustrates the whole process with gestures.] But all of the rest was solid. They'd begin to hew it out, but for fear they hew too deep in de wood, they made a few auger holes then. And they could keep checkin' the depth to keep from going through. When they'd get those log boats made, it'd take about two or three, or a wagon or something, to get them to the pond. It's unusual anybody kept 'em locked. They handled real good in de water and—they were not hard to paddle, really better than the boats now, made outta lumber. And those few auger holes, they'd take cypress and make pegs and drive 'em in solid and smooth 'em off. And sometimes if you didn't check on it real close, you'd never know they had been put in there.

Then they come in with a boat made out of juniper lumber. [A member of the cypress family, this tree has cones and has leaves that resemble needles.] Lawton Huggins had one when I first started to work. And the bottom of that boat—they didn't have it the long way; they had de lumber crossways, from the sides near on. He threw it out there in the sun for two or three days, or a week or two, and they'd be cracks in it the size of this chair all around [leans and points toward bottom of incliner]. Then if you wanted to use the boat, you had to throw it in the pond overnight and it would swell up. Now if you made that boat with dry lumber and put it together good and tight, it was going to swell and buckle up. So those people then, they had a art.

[How did he get the job of game warden?] Well, the Good Lord has looked after me. He's never furnished me no wealth, but I've had ideal friends. There came up a vacancy. [His patron was a family friend, Mr. H.M. Eliot.] I don't know whether they gave it to me to starve me or how [smiles]. But anyway he helped me to get on. I would have started in the fall of forty-nine with one exception—the county was broke. [He and Catherine share a laugh.] So they had to wait till some of the money come in.

I remember the No-Fence Law[41] and I started to school at six years old. In the winter months I'd get up 'fore day and walk from here—you know where Buford's at over there—and the roads kind of zigzagged and made it further. [He gestures throughout the story.] It was the same branch at Cedar Creek; it originates here. Gapway [Swamp] goes right back this a-way, and Cedar Creek goes this way [gestures], and we were just on de dividing line. We could have made canal ditches and turned the water movement either way. But between here and Duford we had to cross [on foot-logs] three times. We crossed at de Grantham Farm and circled around where Rafe Grainger's—do you know John D. Hook's place? Come back in just this side of de church, follows down, and then cuts across down there at d'other side of the Jim Anderson farm [gestures].

When I started work, they had a county fish and game commission. And they didn't expect you to work part-time, they expected you to work all the time. [Smiles.] [Later] they expected us to work a half a day on Sunday. But if they were extremely liberal, if you wanted to go to church on Sunday morning, then you'd expect to go to work that afternoon [chuckles].

They gave us the laws, and we'd discuss—you were kinda on y'own. Then you would discuss different things with d' mag'strate and you knowed what people liked or didn't like. And most of the folks didn't like fish-trapping. And it was right comical—a fellah over here in Causey, he write to A. Richardson and ask him was it legal to set up a fish trap on his own land. And Mr. Richardson wrote him back and told him, "No, it wasn't against the law to set fish traps on his own *land*, but make sure he didn't put none in the *water*." [Much laughter.]

[They review the history of the South Carolina Wildlife Commission, founded in 1952, up to which time Gary had to furnish his own boat and motor. Then Catherine asks about wardens who had been shot.] I know what it is to look down a gun barrel and tell a fellah, I says, "I don't believe you'll shoot. You just as well give me the gun." At about like from here to the gentleman over here [points to Wells] and as I made a step toward him—I didn't get hurt—I made the step, I see him get tense [jerks to his left]. So then I says, "Well, what happened?" He never would give me his squirrel, but I'd take the warrant to have him up in high court. But by recommending mercy for him, it put him under a two-year suspension, I believe it was, and a hundred-dollar fine where normally the fine would have been twenty-five dollars.

[Repeat offenders?] A good many of 'em. I remember one feller—and I, in a way, liked him; and I might have caught him more than anybody else. But he made a living on the river at Sandy Bluff fishin' [on the Little Pee Dee] and drove a Chrysler while I was driving a Plymouth. Without any schoolin'. [How?] Fish Traps.[42]

[They discuss the history of Pee Dee Baptist Academy. A high school held in Wannamaker School, then Wannamaker Church, it was founded by state and local Baptists in 1921—just in time for Gary and Doug and five years before the creation of state-supported consolidated rural schools.[43] Gary later tells a story about the construction of the academy's own building in the 1920s, a long-abandoned but handsome frame structure next to Wannamaker Church; he says that a white foreman would vehemently curse the "'niggers layin' brick,'" and in turn they would giggle at him around a corner of the building as if it was a game. Catherine laughs politely, then asks Doug about the flood of 1928, which pushed water from the Lumber River between him and the train station.]

Bailey: I was going back to the university in the fall with two other boys. We usually got on a train in Loris [from Myrtle Beach] and we had to change in Chadbourn [North Carolina, the junction with the train from Wilmington to Columbia] and come back toward Mullins. But we found out the water was too high, so someone in Loris carried us by automobile near Nichols [like Mullins, in Marion County]. So Joe Grainger had a boat there, and he was taking people across the river into town. But you couldn't catch a train except in Mullins, so we walked there down the railroad track or somewhere or another. We had a small suitcase apiece and spent the night in a hotel. We acted like ten- or twelve-year-old boys. We had pillow fights and everything else that night! [Laughs.]

Mincey: We had a picture of the railroad track. It was taken in front of the Battle Store [in Nichols], where the water must have been eight or ten inches deep in it. Doug should tell you about Old Bawl and d' night we went coon huntin' [laughs].

Bailey: I wanted to take a bunch of th' boys coon-huntin' with me from school, so they all came one night and went down to what we called Gapway Swamp towards Causey. Time we got to the woods, my dog started trailing. He ran the prettiest you ever saw, and sat down at the tree and just treed him so beautifully, you know. [Looks up at an imagined canopy.] I was so proud of him, and these boys who'd never been hunting with him before, they'd just hug him. So we'd have an axe; had it up a large oak—a green oak—I mean a large one, too. We cut that oak. [Pause, smiles.] And we didn't get a coon. I was embarrassed to death. [Shakes head.] I told Papa about it, he said, "Well, the trees were real thick and of course coons will jump one tree to the other [lifts opened hands]. Sometimes they might not be up the tree that he'd treed. But we stayed out and hunted all night and came out at Causey, didn't we, Gary?"

Mincey: We came out at old Causey Schoolhouse—Douglas had forgot that there's ever been a old schoolhouse in Causey.[44]

111

Doug, Catherine and Gary.

Bailey: They had a commissary over there for the hands [of a timber operation]. So I found out about it, and we'd grow a lot of watermelons; so I got me a new wagon one day and I loaded some right by myself. I don't think Papa even knew about it. Went to Causey. And I sold those things just about as fast as I could hand 'em out. They were buying those watermelons fifty cent apiece. Oh, I was getting rich. I was making me some money! So I took another load, not too long after that, and they were glad to get them again. They asked me, "Don't you have something else you want to sell?" I said, "Yeah, we got chickens." [Laughs.] They said, "Bring us some chickens!" So Mama agreed for me to take some over there and sell.[45]

I have never had anybody refuse me to hunt on their land. Of course, people are a little bit more peculiar now because there's more hunters than there used to be and game is scarcer now. Your father [Davis O. Heniford, b. 1894 or 1895, d. 1965, a pharmacist who bought Loris Drug Store in 1922] and Mr. Brown were the first ones that ever took me quail hunting. On the farm we didn't have any quail dogs; we had coon dogs. So when I went with them into quail hunting, I thought to myself, "Now this is what I want. This is what I like." Of course back then game was so plentiful, it's almost unbelievable t' tell people how many birds you could kill in those days.

Your father and Mr. Brown 'n I were going down to Wortham's Crossing [the ferry across the Waccamaw River above Highway 9] to hunt and fish, too. I was sittin' in the back seat with a long-barrel, single-barrel gun, and the first thing we knew, up ahead of us there was a big drove of turkeys right in the road. It looked like ten or twelve. They stopped the car right quick and both of 'em started loading their guns and I just stepped out the back. It didn't take me but a second to load my gun and I fired on a turkey [aims an imaginary gun], and they all flew [raises hands and spreads them apart]. Dr. Heniford and Mr. Brown didn't get after me, but I know they felt like it. What they had planned to do was load their guns and drive right up to the turkeys, get out, and get a shot; and I didn't know that. It was the first time I'd ever seen any wild turkeys, so we didn't get one.

[Catherine asks him to tell the story about how he got to Loris after graduation from Pee Dee Baptist Academy.]

I was on the farm, and I had been told in high school that any boy could go to college that wanted to, or girls, that there was always a way to provide it. And I said, "Well, that suits me. I don't mind working." We had a large family and times were hard. You probably didn't have any money. So I said, "Well, I know I'll go to college because there'd be plenty of ways I can work my way through." But the time come, I didn't have that money to contact the college or have the principal to. "Well, you're going to have to have so much money to get started; but you can get enough to come up and get matriculated, and we'll try to help you find a job so you can work your way through." But we didn't raise the money, so I just had to give up. The rest of my classmates got ready to go on to college. Edgar Stanley's wife Golda—you know, her sisters lived next door to us—she and Ed had visited Loris and told Dr. Heniford that I didn't have a chance to go to college. I think they must have recommended me to him to work in the drugstore, so he came to see me.

I was picking cotton, and he and Ed come aside and asked me if I'd like to come to work for him in the drugstore. I said, "Yes, sir. Yes, sir," or words to that effect. [Smiles.] Father wasn't home that afternoon, and I went in the house and talked to my mother about it. She cried; she hated to see me to go but thought it the best thing. [Here he retells the rest of the story just in case it was lost while another videotape was being inserted.] When we got to Loris, I got out at Edgar Stanley's; that's where Dr. Heniford was renting to at that time and got me a room there. He said, "Mr. Stanley's daughter will take you to the drugstore in the morning and make you acquainted with the other clerks," which she did. Dr. Heniford went hunting that morning. He came in about one o'clock, and I was glad to see him. But he was pretty firm; he didn't have much to say [laughs]. But he was a fine person.

So I worked on with him all that year. All of a sudden one day he asked me, "How would you like to go to college?" I said, "Well, I've always wanted to go to college." He said, "How would you like to study pharmacy?" And I said, "What I've seen of it, I think I'd like to be a pharmacist." He said, "Well, if you want to go, I'll send you." [Shakes head.]

Well, I just couldn't take that in. A man that's no relation to me, and had me there 'n looking after me, gave me a job right off the farm, and then to offer to send me to college—. So he sent me to college four years, and I'm thankful for it. I've often wondered what would have ever happened to me if he hadn't.

[Catherine begins to take leave by thanking the interviewees.]
Mincey: I consider it a honor myself. I was just glad to have you all come. I just regret living here nearly six years now alone 'n everything's going down. [His wife, Ethel Pearl Jones Mincey, had died in 1984.] Well, age is kind of bearing down on me now and this is a pleasure. I've had eighty-three birthdays. I was born February 20, nineteen and seven. I've got nearly three months on him.

Bailey: But I tell you [points], Gary is strongest man I know of for his age. When you can get in a boat and go up and down the river by yourself—fish by yourself all hours of the day and sometime at night.

Mincey: [Smiles.] When I was in m' upper teens, I'd back up the wagon get a two-hundred-pound bag of fertilizer right and carry it. [Lifts imaginary bag.] We didn't know about twenty-four and one-hundred-and-twenty-five-pound bags. And we'd have to step two or three rows across to drop them off where we'd pile it. I'm not sure that I couldn't carry a two-hundred-pound bag of fertilizer now on my back.

Bailey: I believe he could. [How long has he been at Loris Drugstore?] Came in 1925. Been there every year since, except the four years I was in college.

Mincey [points to his own head]: I shouldn't hesitate to say; my weakness is up here. [Laughter.][46]

S.F. Horton.

S.F. Horton

Born 1911

"If any boy can excel at anything, it helps him with everything."

Mr. Salathiel F. Horton grew up in Chesterfield County, and after graduating from Clemson University in 1932, he moved to Williamsburg County to teach vocational agriculture in Greeleyville. After a year he was transferred to Loris, where in 1946 he went into the agricultural supply business. During his career he not only brought education to farmers but farmers to education by encouraging many young men to attend Clemson.

In June 1990 Catherine Lewis interviewed her fellow Loris resident at his home at 5520 Main Street, Loris, next door to Douglas Bailey, longtime owner of Loris Drug Store. Sitting amid awards from his alma mater and photographs of his grandchildren was "S.F.," "Horton," "Horty" or "Squire Horton" (a salutation accorded to a gentleman farmer, explains Professor Prince, who reviewed this chapter). A handsome man with gray hair and black-framed glasses, he spoke clearly in a measured pace, and he emphasized points by tilting his head.

The author thanks S.F.'s son Lewis for making corrections to this chapter. See also *IRQ* 22.1 (1988), an issue devoted to the people, places and events of Loris.

Livestock has been a big part of our program here over the years, as long as I taught. We had put twenty-seven registered Guernsey bulls in the Loris High School district, most all of them from Chesterfield County. I knew the people and there was a good many good cows there so I could get bull calves just for the asking almost—veal prices. We had a good bull in walking distance of every farm—beef-type and dairy type—that if a feller wanted to get into the business—and a good many of them did.

Joe Blount was considered one of the best farmers we had in the Loris District. He was an outstanding tobacco farmer and had four children but he didn't have a milk cow. I kept working with him and he finally got him a cow and a nice barn for it and the calf. He raised his calf, he beefed it and he canned it for the family. Had him a spicket [spigot] and everything in his barn to get water for his cows. But anyway, his cow died, and he came to me and wanted to know if I knew where he could get one, he wanted to get him another cow to*day*. And he told me there had been so much improvement in the health and appearance of his children that he couldn't afford not to have him a cow.

It was common for people here not to have cows. They just wasn't in the area. One tobacco season I brought in fifty-six milk cows. That was during the war [World War II] years—meat and butter was rationed and people had the money and they could make good biscuits without any lard and meat if they had butter. I just went to Chesterfield County and on to Charlotte, and brought 'em in, brought fifty-six during one tobacco season.

One of the boys that I think has been a right outstanding citizen—as far as just a old country boy come up—was John Hardee that sells insurance. His people had been sort of average farmers, nothing extryordinary. And he had a bad impediment of speech; he was just shy and you couldn't get anything much out of him [as a student]. I told [the superintendent] I thought that John was doing pretty well in agriculture, that he had got him a nice heifer calf that I located for him somewhere. He was looking forward to raising him a cow, had him a pasture program goin'. I imagine John Hardee is worth half a million dollars. He's a insurance representative, owns the store at Mount Vernon, and he's a *smooth talker*. You know, if any boy can excel at anything, it helps him at *everything*. And he found out that there was some things he could do as well as other people. And he just got to doing it actually better than a lot of other people.

Success and the nice homes you see in Horry County now is not all the result of agricultural teaching in the schools here in Loris, but you see the farm program—where tobacco was averaging eight to ten cents a pound then, it's a dollar and a half to a dollar-seventy-five now. But there had to be some leaders who promoted the program.

I visited a fellow near Loris the first year I was here that had tobacco and it was selling, as I said, cheap. He was a sharecropper and there was very few packhouses. People would crop their green tobacco and cure it, then just take a bedroom and take down the beds [gestures] and pile up the tobacco. Whenever they closed the warehouses to try to get the history of each individual's farming operation, it took a week or two or three that the houses didn't operate. But this fellow said to his landlord, "Captain, when you goin' to open up these warehouses and let us get rid of some of this tobacco?" Said, "We've already had to take down all of our beds, sleepin' on the floor," and said, "I done slept on the floor so much my hips is done riz twice." [He and Catherine laugh.]

[Catherine asks about the Simpson Creek Drainage Project, the attempt to channel a large swamp system east of Loris that flows into the Waccamaw above Red Bluff.] It was the first of its kind in the nation, is my understanding. And that happened after the war was over and Lewis Carter [b. 1907], a Loris boy, came here. Those farmers met and met and met and they divided up, 'cause there was some federal aid, too, and you see, there wasn't any federal aid when I was teaching. But under this Soil Conservation Program the farmers could pool their allocation on a drainage project. They worked out the closeness to the creek. They figured that a fellow's farm was more valuable [with better drainage], and as you come way on up the hill, they assessed him less, but they worked it out systematically and everybody agreed to it. They put the project in and got the [Army Corps of Engineers]. They surveyed it out and built the project. You see, your roads and your upland would all flood when the water couldn't get down the creek. It was a remarkable thing for the area and it's been others patterned after the project. And that record is in the Hall of Fame Agriculture Department in Washington, the whole program of the Simpson Creek Drainage.

[Seed-cleaning?] After I resigned from [the position of] the agriculture teachers' "head," you might say, at Loris, in 1946, I went in with Mr. Harry Lewis—who operated the warehouse, sold fertilizer, tobacco flues, hail insurance—with the understanding that I could add other things to the line. Seed was a right long suit with me and we handled a right good bit of it. And I got—we did—to be a distributor for Coker Pedigreed Seed Company and got at least one local grower here to grow pedigreed seed for Coker.[47] I put in a seed cleaner to process the seed, grown under Coker's supervision, and then I was gon' distribute it. And then [the farmers] wouldn't have to go into Hartsville [headquarters of the company]. Coker supervised the growing but I put in a modern seed cleaner, which was the first one.

Incidentally, it was made by the Clipper seed-cleaning people 'n had been sold as a new machine to a feller in Kershaw County to clean crotalaria.[48] On sandy land, it [this plant] grew and the seed was shipped widely for building land. Well, it was found then that the crotalaria seed gettin' into a chicken feed, for example, would kill the chicken. So they outlawed crotalaria as a crop, and his machine was sittin' up there in perfect condition and not used in two or three years. I found out about it and went up there 'n bought it and brought it to Loris and it's still in use. Whenever I got out of the business, I sold to Bill Page, who is running the Page Chemical Company now, and that's one of the principal items in his total line of business, his custom cleaning and cleaning certified seed. And as a result of gettin' into the seed-cleaning business, I was on the Crop Improvement and the Foundation Seed Boards at Clemson. I'm on the Crop Improvement Board now. I reckon I've been on one or the other or both for twenty-five to thirty years.[49]

But good seed—I planted one row of stuff in my garden this year that not one seed [raises index finger] come up on its own row. I took pride when I was selling seed to have 'em tested and *know* what I was doing. People came far and wide—I'm not trying to crow—but Mrs. Floyd Worley came in one day (they lived over in Nichols and bought their fertilizer out of Loris), she said, "Mr. Horton, it's about that time of year again." They would come to Loris go get the seed because it's somethin' awful for a fellow to go out there and take a hundred-foot or a hundred-yard row, level it up and dig his holes and put them in the ground by hand and not a one come up.

[The future of the family farm?] No, it don't look good to me. Without a young fellow can come up in a farm family and inherit it, I don't think in the last fifteen or twenty years, it has been possible for a fellow in Horry County to start out from scratch. The old system used to be he was hired laborer for a while, then he would maybe get married and move up to a sharecropper, and then he would buy him a piece of land and become a landowner. You can't go that route now. There is no way on earth with the interest as high as it is, and land as high as it is, for a fellow to buy a farm and pay for it off of the farm. He's got to be a part-time farmer or he's got to inherit it, or he's got to marry it, one or the other. He can't come up the ladder like he used to.

[He praises earlier agricultural teachers J.H.Yon, R.E. Naugher and M.J. Bullock.] The year I [taught in Greeleyville, South Carolina] I had the smallest number of boys of any teacher in South Carolina. And the first year I came to Loris, I had the most boys of any teacher in South Carolina on account of the fact that our high school district covered a large area. We had eighteen of these little grammar school districts, feeder schools, and it was a high percentage of the population was white. Where I had just come from in Williamsburg County, two-thirds were black.

Gilbert [Hardee] was, I guess, the outstanding agriculture student by all measurements that Loris ever had. He told me that at the time he was in the service, in the Navy NCO [Non-commissioned Officer] leadership training at Bambridge, Maryland, in his course in public speaking, he chose as a topic this rural electricity and what it meant to the standard of living for the farm family. It had come in, of course, all since I had been to Loris. We went around as agriculture teachers and tried to encourage the farmers to sign up so they'd have enough patrons on each line to justify building the lines.

[When the videotape of the 1990 interview was declared lost after a thorough search, Catherine reacted without complaint and conducted another session in May 1991, motivated in part by her fascination with early farming practices. Luckily the first tape reappeared, but this bonus interview provides even more firsthand details.]

Well, the chief cash crop of course was tobacco, as it is today. And it was farmed by individuals on small ownership farms. A high percentage at that time of the farmers were small and white and a lot of the older ones then had not had much opportunity to go to school. Your daddy told me that he went to a little two- or three-teacher school right up here where the Dairy Maid is and there was not a paved road leadin' into Loris from any direction when I came here. You had to ride on the dirt to get to Loris. [Catherine laughs.] There was no rural electricity and most of the rural houses were not painted and screened.

The people were of course thrifty. I never saw as many hogs slaughtered for home use, nor as good of gardens [chuckles], and especially collards in the winter. And then they had the access to the fish on the beach. And they grew the corn and potaters. They fared well as far as eating, but very *few* had livestock except hogs and chickens and no cows much, and very few milk cows.

They had me to show a map one time in Columbia at a state agriculture teachers' convention of our high school district, which is larger than Dillon County. But I had a dairy-type and a beef-type bull in walking distance to every farm in the high school district, and a lot of 'em—even some of our better farmers, just never bothered themselves to have a milk cow. Joe Blount told me that they'd rather *buy* milk, but I told them that they would buy it as long as the babies was on the bottle but if they didn't have a milk cow whenever they quit using the bottle, they didn't have any milk.

Well, the average acreage of tobaccer would have been four acres or less, I would say. There was a lot of land, but a lot of it was not cleared and drained. Just like it's gettin' back to be now: we've got land lyin' out in. I have it myself—it's good land, now—but you can't make any money on corn and soybeans—sharecropping it, and people won't pay you anything for cash-rentin' it, so there wasn't much incentive for a feller to go out there and work hard.

Corn sold. At these little old grocery stores, people would bring it and sell it for as little as fifty cent a bushel; and whenever I started to work with 'em for feeding hogs, I told them they could get more money for the corn. Some of them was a little slow to cotton on the idea and I insulted a bunch of them one time down here at Simpson Creek one night. Your daddy might have been with me when I was talking to them. I told them it suited me all right for 'em to bring the corn up here to Loris and sell it, that I was buying it, and that I would buy a hundred bushels at a time from Mr. Turner that run a little feed store. I had me a little [corn] crib and he would send his boys up there and fill up my homemade feeders and put the other half in the barn and I could use that when he got out of corn. I told the farmers that if they didn't believe it, I could show 'em the figures that I was making more on the corn without touchin' it than they sold it for—not what they made, what they sold it for. So a good many of them started to feeding hogs.

One bunch, not too far from your time, Paul Boyd—I had him in school and he had a nice place right in front of his house, pecan grove [circles with hand]—and I told him that if he would keep the feed and water to some hogs, I'd put some down there, furnish all the money, and if we made any profit, we'd split it. Bought some rough-looking feeder pigs from Mr. Sam Graham, and the word got out; a good many fellows was interested in buyin' during the war years for growin' out their own meat. I went down there and I told 'em that I didn't need any hogs to kill, I had plenty and that they got there before I did and if any of them wanted the pigs at the price, they were welcome to 'em. I said, "Let's ask Mr. Graham what

Nicotiana tabacum.

he wants for dese pigs." So he told us he wanted to pick out about ten or fifteen of them, the sorriest ones he had at four or five dollars apiece, and I asked the farmers if any of them wanted them. "No, siree, not at that price." I said, "Well, I'll take them." And I put 'em over there and Paul looked after 'em. And me and him made about seventy-five dollars apiece in about seventy-five days, and that was right good money then.

And the neighborhood saw them and Havy Boyd, Paul's daddy, said that somebody told him—they was talkin' about me being involved in feeding hogs and one thing or another—he says, "Horton is interested in making money." Havy said, "Yes," and said, "You'd make some, too, if you'd pay attention." [Laughs.]

I think that teaching agriculture is designed primarily for young, energetic people. After a fellow gets so old [chuckles], I don't think he's got much business. In fact in the last week a former student of mine told a group at the Masonic Hall that he had agriculture under me: "I remember well a lot of things we did," he said; "You could go out there and if we wanted to castrate a bull, he could throw him right flat of his back in just a minute." [They laugh.] But an old fellow couldn't do that. [Smiles broadly.]

[Catherine asks about African American teachers in vocational education.] W.P. Johnson was here and then he moved on and got into the extension, but George Cooper was a super individual and a good man to work with. In Williamsburg County, they had a feller—Barr, that was principal of the black school [in Greeleyville] and also a part-time agriculture teacher, and two-thirds of the population in that area was black. There wasn't many white people in my area, and I worked with him and his people as much or more than I did with the white people. Barr was super.

Another thing about Williamsburg County: they had been so many black people until those white people just depended on them to do the work. They were trifling. The white people wouldn't work. A sharecropper would talk about his "plowboys." [They share a laugh.] And I didn't have no desire to stay down there, but when I got to Loris I never saw as hard a working and as industrious a group of white people anywhere else in my life. They would *all* work. And they figured that was the way to get ahead. That's one thing I liked and that's one thing that caused me to want to stay here.

[He gives more details about the Simpson Creek drainage project.] No, I don't think it would be possible to do such a project again. Now they've turned the thing around and gone to talkin' about wetlands. If you go to a state soil conservation meeting and talk about drainage, they'll throw you out of d' office. [But] as far as I am personally concerned, the first year that I worked tobaccer on land that had been tile-drained [by underground pipes], I believe I made five hundred dollars to the acre more than anybody in a mile of me. Yes, good land and I had the land in small grain the year before. All that stubble was turned under and I had the tobacco on high beds and I had it tiled; the water could get into it and work its way into the tile. Where a lot of people's tobacco just drowned, mine fared good.

It is hard for me [to accept the idea that a swamp is valuable]. If you can drain that swamp and grow food and feed, I think it'll eventually have to be done to feed the world.[50]

Andrew Stanley.

Andrew Stanley

Born 1903

"He put me across the river when I was driving the mail."

In April of 1991, Mr. Andrew Stanley was still working his farm. It was located at 2404 Old Chesterfield Road in an area called Wampee, on Highway 90 between the Waccamaw River and the Intracoastal Waterway opposite North Myrtle Beach. His house, low of ceiling and dark, stood near his birthplace amid fields and the ghost of a garden. Once planted in a former pond, it had borne field peas, corn and greens (collard, turnip, and mustard). With the help of a tractor and a grandson he was about to plant corn, tobacco, peanuts and butter beans. "Andr'" or "And'a," as his friends called him, was a tan, slim man, who wore a mauve sweater and gray hat with a circular rim that extended just over his glasses. One tooth was silver under his gray moustache, and one shoe was cut open to the sock so as to indulge a bad toe. Mr. Stanley was energetic and quick moving, often chewing an imaginary substance and illustrating his words with a stick about three inches in diameter and eighteen inches long.

Andrew had married Annie Bethea from North Carolina, and they had raised nine children, who grew up on the place except for the time during World War II when the federal government converted the area to a bombing range. Some of the children moved to New Jersey, some stayed in the area.

This first of two interviews was conducted in April 1991, partly by the author but mainly by C.B. Berry (b. 1919), a month after Berry himself had been interviewed for the project by Catherine H. Lewis. A surveyor and historian, he had served as the first mayor of Crescent Beach (1956) and the first president of the Horry County Historical Society (1967). His treasury of interviews and family trees, *Berry's Blue Book*, would be published in 2006. Berry had done survey work for the interviewee, and now with Wells as observer, the two men sat in front of the tobacco barn made of irregular-shaped cypress poles (logs) still glued together by the clay that Andrew had daubed back in 1950. Besides turning up vivid new particulars, the interview sometimes resembled a ritual with Berry asking a brief question and Stanley supplying a brief and expected answer, or with Stanley imparting information and Berry validating it (or vice versa).

Professor Prince, who knew Andrew, reviewed this chapter. Jackie Stanley, a former student of the author and the daughter of one of Andrew's older grandnephews, made suggestions and additions based on some oral history work of her own.

[Andrew explains that his father, Henry Stanley, had the contract for mail carrying and hired his son to take letters between the Wampee and Conway post offices—an example of a "star route."]

Chillen was chillen till they were twenty-one, and I was thirteen or fourteen years old, and I drove the mail. Mule and an old road cart about wide as this chair. The mailman to the post office put the mail in a little bag and locked the sack, and I throwed it on my shoulder and carried it to the next postmaster, he unlocked it and got the mail out there, and everybody got the mail to the post office. There wasn't no mailbox in the road no place.

I carried the mail three years and three days. Carry it for a dollar and he'd collect the money and give me fifty cent of it. And I bought my five acres of land there with the fifty cents a day. And I bought that over there for a dollar. I bought ten acres of land. The magistrate couldn't make me a deed for it; my daddy and mother [Helen Livingston Stanley] had the deed made in their name. When I come twenty-one, they went back to the magistrate and changed it in my name. Then I went to paying the taxes on it.

Didn't go to no school. I went there eight days and then one day out here at the Popular School [the official spelling], which is just a little bit as that basket there. My teacher was a fellah by the name of Jesse Ford. No sir, I ain't got [a pretty good education]. I got a whole heap of it up there [points to head] but there ain't none in my hands.

Used to work this land with mules and oxens. In '51 when I put my first tractor in here. I've sowed that fertilizer by hand. Take it out in a bucket, walk down the row and string [?] it down the row. Then when I plant my corn, I took a hoe like this and dug the holes and dropped the corn and then covered it up, and dug another hole and dropped it in, then covered it up [illustrates with a rake]. You had to feed them old mules, and then plant the corn in the field and had to strip that fodder off and save it to feed the mules with.

My daddy was a churcher right long as he lived—he lived till he was ninety-nine—and I come up in church. That Popular Church out there [Popular AME, 8415 Hwy 90], I built that church some years ago. Oh, 'tis way difference in what it is now. The average child—until they were twenty-one they went to church barefooted. And I have a sister and a brother older than me—I've seen my mother take a croker [burlap] bag and make her a dress to go to church with Sunday. Then the director in there raised the collection and never got over nine cent, or eight cent or seven cents. Then Earl, the preacher, he'd walk here from yonder to yonder, from there to there, and he spent the night with some of the members and stayed till Monday morning, and then took a stick and run through his suitcase [lays stick over backward over left shoulder] and toted it right back home. Sometimes he couldn't get here once a month, according to the weather. And there wasn't no ride. [Pauses.] And then everybody in the section went to church that Sunday, but there wasn't many people to go to church. Then they went to Sunday school.

Every now and then they'd have a dinner on a Sad'day, and they had chicken and mutton corn and field peas, and corn bread.[51] And they'd o' had rice 'cause they grew the rice in the field. About every family had rice. Have a special Easter dinner. Have a Chillun Day, too; and everybody little chillum had a speech to say. Call 'em out by name, they'd go up and speak and sit back down till they went 'round [until everyone got a chance to give a speech].

That little road right by my house was the road to go to the beach—the Inland Waterway wasn't there. [It opened in 1936.] Had a little dirt road, little ol' boggy road. Sometime they waded in water that deep and that deep through there; and the branches over the road—you'd stoop your head down [stoops] jam to the beach highway you call Ocean Drive. They called it Windy Hill. This old gentleman by the name of Tom Bell [operated a fishery there]. He had a house out there and a cemetery was right back of his house, pecan orchard like mine. I brought the pecan trees on the mail; we set 'em on his place over there.

I believe there was six in the boat pulling the boat 'round, and then there was fifteen, or seventeen or eighteen sometime on the hill [dune] pulling the net out. They'd give you a share of fish. Dey owner'd get a third, then dey's divide 'em up in shares for the hands. The average of 'em was mullets and spots; you'd catch a few catfish and you'd catch a few—uh—sheepheads [sheepshead, a bony species with broad incisor teeth]. The other, the hogs eat 'em. And then don't put one in your pocket or something, or they let its tail be sticking out—they'd fine you. Give you ten licks for that, or eight licks for that, or four licks for that.

[Our share was] sometime ten pounds, sometimes five pounds, sometime two pound, sometimes one pound. [Because we didn't have ice,] we cooked 'em and ate 'em. And then if I had too many, my mother sent a neighbor some over—they didn't have none. We salt 'em down later. Split 'em, washed 'em, and put 'em in a barrel and put salt on 'em—or you salt 'em as you put 'em in. Took 'em out and put 'em in a tub, and pour water on 'em and soak 'em. Then I had to go way down to the branch, to a spring, to get water to pour in there and soak 'em out. There weren't no pump or well. Spring down yonder side o' the branch—that family got out it, and that family, and the other family and the other family. Then further on over another spring was the same way. All'd tote water up to the house.

[To grind our corn to meal] they had a hand-mill to the house with the two big rocks on top of one another [millstones] and a lever on it with the notches in it. You could drop it down lower, it'd grind you meal [illustrates by holding stick vertically]. Then you'd pick it up higher to make your grits and you turned that 'round and 'round and 'round [circles with stick]. It had a handle that turned it 'round and 'round—a big rock. Then you had a little trough built around your rock 'round there—your meal'd pour out.

Then later hit come a steam boiler down here in Dogwood Neck. Crossed there just below my field over there. And they had a mill that was on Mr. Jet Todd's place. His wife was one of my postmasters that was at Hand Post Office. And we'd carry our corn over there later, and they'd grind it there—do that steam mill. They fired the boiler with wood. The train runned out there. They fired *hit* with wood. [The log train to Conway

Lumber Company on the Waccamaw was operated by Gardner & Lacy Lumber Company.] Grind it for you take so much toll out of it.

We got that cotton gin to Wampee right where the road lean left to go to Tallwood—57 I believe it is. Mr. Hamp Woods ran the cotton gin. He had a grits mill, too. Yeah, it was run by the same boiler. They would use their own wood to heat the boiler, and then there was a whole leaf o' vaircut [heap of vacant] land and nobody'd object 'em of getting the wood off of the land. Tobacco—we'd sit down there on the floor and grade it in three grades—first grade, second grade, third grade. Then when you'd get ready to carry it to the market, you drove a pair of mules up there, or ox and cart, and backed up there and load it and carried it to Conway. And there wasn't but one warehouse in Conway. Then you'd get cotton, you'd load *hit* up in the wagon and carry it to Conway. And the gin was Spivey's gin, I remember it now.

Didn't have no doctors. The baby had to come, but I've never known in my lifetime no lady lossin' her life having a baby. Had midwives. I remember Aunt [?] Caroline Vereen. Lived right close to where I'm living now. Then I remember another old lady named Catherine Randall. Lived way down to Sugar Hill—where they get all that sand from to haul all about. And old lady Caroline lived till she was one hundred and fifteen or sixteen. And then her husband is named Stonewall Jackson Vereen, and he lived till he was one hundred and twelve or thirteen. She delivered many and a many of babies. She delivered *me*. Later, years on after I were grown, about the time I were driving the mill, old gentleman come in here named Tom Bell. The next road past the pastor's is the Star Bluff Road, right there over to your left, and he was the doctor. If you had typhoid fever or malaria fever, he'd come.

I can remember—[if] I'd gi' ya a dollar or ten cent for every automobile come in Conway, you'd make a straight mark in Myrtle Beach. You wouldn't have made na'y [nary] a penny. Now look at it today.

I have children older than that waterway. I worked right where the Inland Waterway is—worked corn, picked cotton in there. I holped clear the right-of-way. I were a grown man then and there wasn't no road at that time to go to Myrtle Beach. You'd zigzag through the woods, brush dragging ya. The average time we'd try to catch the tide down and go to strand [get to the beach at low tide]. Then there was one old company sto' in Myrtle Beach, and there wasn't na'y automobile parked around it, or nowhere. It belonged to Burroughs & Collins. They had a great big old farm down in the swamp, and all grades of mules working in that swamp. There wasn't a tractor in there, and all grades of men and women working in that swamp. They growed beans and string beans, butter beans, corn, uh—rice. A lot of Irish potatoes, a lot of onions, a lot of squashes. Kind of a truck farm, that's right. And didn't have no truck to haul it nowhere; and the old train back up, and then it lef' a car on the railroad, and they'd load it by the time the next train come back. And then the train come back, it'd pick it up and carry it. [Myrtle Beach was] almost nothing. Almost nothing. There wasn't an automobile; and anyone didn't pass through there during the week, or month, or two months, or a year.

[Our houses:] Every one of 'em looked just alike. They looked just like that tobacco barn. Some of 'em had the clay daubed in the crack like that. [Folks] didn't get much paper at that time, but they'd save what they got; and close to Christmas time, they took some flour and mixed it up and made 'em a paste and stuck it all over da inside with paper [to stop the draft].

And the average of 'em had two: had a kitchen and a house. Then lay 'em a board from the house to the kitchen [turns stick to walkway] and walk the board from the house to the kitchen. And everybody made a fire out the do' at night. Then they had a cook-shelf out the door—the crotch under there [stick becomes shelf] and lay it on that, and then another crotch on it. Put the san' up there, straw or something, so the sand wouldn't pour through, and cook up there, put their pots up there. And if it come a bad, rainy evening till late overnight, you had to [words not clear] yourself or you didn't get none![52]

Whenever I were young, there wasn't a white family in this section on this side of the river. It was all black. All the land was b'long to black, and they had no education or nothing. Whole leaf of 'em didn't know a dollar from fifty cent. Then they [white people] would raise a little old yearling and sell that yearling t'em for fifteen dollars, and they had no way to work to pay for 'em direct. They'd take that land for that one little yearling. [He names two white families.] My grandmother was a old lady. She lived till she was one hundred and twelve or one hundred and thirteen, and she owned it from the other side of that pecan tree yonder to the Star Bluff Road. Then she had a brother named Prince Livingston. He caught it from her there, and he went to Wampee Branch and crossed the Waccamaw River in places over there. Now the family owned about fifty yards of it. [Silence.]

[How did the blacks come to own all this land?] When the freedom from the slavery—they sot 'em out over here. And blazed a blade through there with a knife, said, "Now, that's yours, Dean," and "That's your own, So-and-so," and "That's yours." They then'd cut another streak, "And that's yours, Kit," "And that's yours, Martha," and that's the way they went. There wasn't no surveyor, no plat or nothing.

[Wells and Stanley had little in common besides their birthday—February 13—but they got along well. So the author did a follow-up interview in October 1993, while his family waited in the car, hostages to history. After transcribing the audiotape, he drove back to Wampee and read the pages aloud to Mr. Stanley, who volunteered a few additions. In 2006 the author listened to the tape again and modified his own transcription.]

'Cross the river? I had a little old boat with a paddle and somebody live right across the river there and take me across every day. Then bring me 'cross every day. [Donnie Grant?] I know him well. He put me across the river when I was driving that mail a million a million a million days. Everybody in this section knew him as Link Vereen. He's fifteen years older than me. I was—fourteen or fifteen years old.[53]

Oh, yeah! I've been in to see about my cows 'n my pigs 'n my chickens and things. I ain' been straddlin' no tractor this morning, today's Sunday. I believe in my Lord, now. That's who blessed me to live so long. But now tomorrow morning this time, I'll be doing something else with a tractor or be diggin' potatoes or something.

My grandmother was kinda small—dark-skinned, slim lady, smoked a pipe all the time. Cooked out the door all her life. And she could raise sheeps and she'd sham [shear] 'em. My grandpa was a Bessent [Jim].[54] I feels all right about it. He was a quiet man. He was nice. He'd visit my daddy, I seen him layin' in my daddy's bed. I appreciate it right on. I didn't look it too much, but now I have some children look it, and my brother, he has some children look it. My sister has some children; they look it, but I come out on my mother's side more. But I was happy with it. I *still* happy with it. And my daddy, now, you couldn't hardly tell the difference in the color o' you and him. [Were racial relationships amicable?] No, no, sir! It was rough—they didn't want you around, they'd beat you and feed ya out the door like a dog if you worked for 'em. Changed now, they're just as nice as they can be. I'm glad of dis.[55]

I was trained different 'cause my daddy had a white daddy. Then he'd visit him, and he'd pat me and rub my head—sometimes he'd give me a little penny—I thought the world of him.

[Does he remember any kind white people?] Well...[long pause]. I can 'member a few was—was different from the other. They'd feed 'em and give 'em things. A white lady [Sarah Edge] give me the first suit of clothes I've ever worn. Yup, dey all wasn't alike; some of 'em was nice. Just like it is today—some of 'em is nice and some black is nice 'n some of 'em ain't.

Julia Pryor Macklen.

Julia Pryor Macklen

Born 1902

"I think we did our gambling when we got here."

If S.F. Horton was an early leader in cows, hogs and seeds, Julia Pryor Macklen was a pioneer of pies.

Shortly after Mr. S.F. returned to Loris to become a catalyst for improvement in agriculture, Julia and her husband H. Lloyd Macklen arrived in Horry County to become influential figures in tourism—not only in business and but also in promotion. Raised on a farm in Enterprise, near the Waccamaw River halfway between Socastee and Bucksport, Lloyd met Julia in Greenville, North Carolina, where she taught school and he worked on a construction job. In 1935 the Macklens bought a grocery store in Myrtle Beach and eventually operated Lloyd's Motor Hotel and Restaurant. Facing Kings Highway, the complex occupied all the land between Sixteenth and Seventeenth Avenues North, with the Piggly Wiggly store across the street to the north and Chapin Memorial Park to the south.[56] The Macklens' endeavor made little distinction between family and business: "Employees were treated better than I was," remembered their son Robert Pryor Macklen; "I worked seven days a week from age twelve till college."

Catherine Lewis conducted the interview on March 25, 1993, at Julia's home, 3600 N. Kings Highway, a corner where she gave the author a tour of her flower gardens when he visited once or twice with a videotape or transcription. At the time of the interview she was the oldest member of the First United Methodist Church (which had begun as a cottage), but she still spoke with a South Georgia accent.

The transcript was annotated by Mrs. Macklen soon after it was typed, and in 2006 her son Robert made additions that appear in the endnotes with his initials. This chapter was also reviewed by Dr. J. Marcus Smith Sr.

He had taken me to Georgia to have my fourth child [Robert, b. 1935] where my mother could help and take care of me, and on his way back he stopped to see his brother, who had a complete grocery store, including seafood. His brother said that Chapin's [for decades the main emporium in town] was building a place [at 803 Main St.] across from them where they were going to open a seafood place in competition with him. So he talked his brother into renting it, which he did. I think the store had really been built to sell because Lloyd's brother, Clarence, had a complete grocery and seafood store that was very competitive to Chapin's and getting a lot of their business.[57] Patricia Manor was going and was the most popular place I would say at Myrtle Beach.[58] For the elite. Lloyd was competitive and began to carry other food items. He spent many hours in his truck and in Wilmington, North Carolina, waiting for trucks to arrive at daybreak that had vegetables, fruits, and seafoods that were not available at his brother's store. Turnips, rutabagas and cabbage grown here had previously been all the vegetables available here. Chapin's did not carry fowl or seafood. Lloyd practiced offering only the best of everything that was available in his store. Good service was stressed. All written charges required the signature of the buyer, and payment was expected by the end of the week.[59]

One day as Lloyd was driving to Myrtle Beach from Conway, he thought of something that pleased him so highly that he almost had a car accident. "Lloyd's of London insures everything. Lloyd's of Myrtle Beach assures prices, quality, and service." Soon afterwards this was printed on his store's window. Later two men from New York City saw that sign, came into the store, and told Lloyd that sign was next to the best sign they had ever seen, which was Wrigley's Chewing Gum sign in New York City.

You knew practically everyone here. In many respects it was delightful. The principal of the school [H. K. Sanders] and his wife had no children [until the mid-forties] and they became very fond of mine and often brought them from the school just to have them be with 'em.

I had a black woman who stayed there during the day and helped me, and sometimes that was really terrible because you can't govern someone, you know, when you are away from them. But one day I got ready to go to the PTA meeting and pulled my one good dress down to put it on and it was black all around the neck. I knew that she had been taking my dress home with her, wearing it, bringing it back, and hanging it up in the closet. So I did not go to the PTA for that meeting. [Chuckles.] But I got rid of her and got the best colored woman to help me, Jessie. I could trust her with the children and she seemed to be happy with them.[60]

We rented a very small house that had been the house for the man who was the caterer, or the manager, of the food department of the Ocean Forest Hotel.[61] It was built very well but didn't have anything but regular bathroom facilities and of course a sink and water in the kitchen. But no central heat or cooling. And we had a little stove in the living room that I don't think it was more than fourteen inches in diameter where the heat came from and you burned up one side and froze on the other. [Smiles.]

And by [the time we moved after a few years,] I had five children. For the help in the store, Mack had employed two young men who were working in the summer to make it possible for 'em to pay for going to college. They stayed in the house where we were living in, that small house. And me and my husband and five children—and a sister of mine came to manage the cash in the store, she was there, too. And I cooked with the help of a black woman that I'd brought from Georgia and served three meals every day from that place. Those two young men who had been in the store, at the end of the summer they said, "Mrs. Macklen, I don't think that Patricia Manor even served as good food as you have fed us all summer."[62]

No, I had no authority about that [venturing into the restaurant business]. In fact my husband never asked me about what he was planning to do, he just did it and I guess I survived all right. So hard work won't kill ya. [Laughs.].

I used to make six quarts of fresh ice cream, homemade, with all the ingredients of a dozen eggs and all that cream and stuff—*every single Sunday* for all the help. [Laughs.] And it was made out of what fresh fruit you know was going to spoil if we didn't sell it.

We sold the grocery business before Mack bought the motel. Actually I was at home and he was riding with Mr. [John] McLeod, who was a big Realtor at the time, a very fine person. And Mack didn't know what he wanted to do. They passed one of the first two motor courts at Myrtle Beach—Travelers Motor Hotel—which had about twenty-four rooms and baths and with a nice center arrangement that was attractively planted.[63] So Mr. McLeod said, "There is something that's for sale." And so Mack said, "Well, Mr. McLeod, write the people and ask 'em how much I would need to pay them to move into it." He did and we moved into that motor hotel. And it was a wonderful business. It was in such demand because with having only two there, they were seen on the Highway [Kings Highway]. [Sometimes] we could sit down in our living room, which was our office, and see the cars slow down and then go on; and we would realize that we had failed to turn the sign from "No vacancy" to "Vacancy," and we could fill up in a matter of a few hours.[64]

But listen to this. [Pauses.] All of a sudden there was a man staying with us. This man and his wife built a motor hotel and a restaurant. And they weren't in it hardly two years before they were ready to get out and talked my husband into buying it and selling Travelers. Actually there were times when I really regretted not leaving him when he made me do that. [Catherine laughs.] Because there we had these wonderful people that we served and a lovely place to stay, comfortable, with steam heat and cooling—and to get into a restaurant that I knew nothing about and he knew nothing about. But I guess I lived as well as a queen almost in my home because although there were so many of us, we had anything that was the desire of most wealthy people.[65]

You wouldn't believe how cheap it was written on that menu. I think you could get toast and coffee and one egg for about thirty-five cents. It was ridiculous. And we served things that they don't serve now. We were lucky because everybody needed somethin' to get money for; we had colored men and white people to bring us wonderful food. Someone would go fishing, for instance, just to have something to do, and catch more fish than they wanted, and they'd bring 'em to our kitchen to sell. Then we could dress them and serve the very best.

I've known of people bringing a whole twenty-four-pound size flour sack full of shelled, fresh butterbeans and lot of delicacies like that that other people had never known about. And I did a lot of salad work for the restaurant. We served fresh fruit salad and we served shrimp and other kind of salads. I was very flattered one day, this nice-looking lady who had just eaten a meal there asked to be introduced to me. So she came on the salad porch and talked to me. She said, "I have traveled all over Europe several times and I have never eaten a salad dressing as delicious as you served on my fruit salad today. And if I was younger, I would ask you to go in business with me and we'd put that salad dressing on the market and make a million dollars." [She and Catherine laugh.]

[The restaurant seated] close to one hundred and fifty or two hundred. We had two dining rooms and the kitchen had glass doors that you could look into the kitchen from where you were seated to eat. Yes, [we operated year-around]. The guests were people going north and south to Florida. It was just amazing how many nice people we had. No [we didn't really have an off-season]. We operated equally as well, if not better.

It was that caramel nut cake [for which she was famous]. You see, I melt sugar, which makes the caramel. And I never test it at all now because I use the same stove, the same eyes [burners], the same pots and each container. 'Cause you have the melted sugar over here [she gestures] and you have this boiling syrup—that has the milk and the sugar and the butter in it—and when that gets melted and it's the same temperature as that, you mix them and add the nuts after you've beaten it a while and spread it. But no one seems to catch on to how to do it. [Catherine laughs.] Although I tell them exactly what I do.

My husband was working to make Myrtle Beach better every minute of the day and night. He would do *anything*. He drove literally thousands of miles [shakes head] trying to sell the town, and every new customer that he met he wanted to tell them about it. At the first meeting of executives in Myrtle Beach, he got up and said, "We have got to advertise! People don't know about us being here and how wonderful it is." He convinced the [president of Myrtle Beach Farms] at that time to start advertising, he'd already put some advertisements from Myrtle Beach probably to Georgetown, telling about our place. Nothing really big, but small signs to indicate that this was a good place to stop overnight.

I would say that he was [instrumental in forming the Chamber of Commerce]. And he was an official of that probably every year. He taught the owners of Chapin Co., which was considered *the* business of Myrtle Beach at the time, to advertise, which they had never done before. [At this point the fourth and last original videotape of the set was missing, and no VHS copy was readily available, so the balance of this chapter has no annotations as to voice and gesture.]

It certainly did [make a lot of difference in traffic after Kings Highway was paved, by 1941].[66] There were times when maybe the weather was so severe that you'd get such a crowd that it would be a little hard to serve them in the manner you prefer to serve them.

We had white waitresses all of the time, never had anything else. But Mack had some very professional caterers that we employed from time to time and they didn't want to be told anything about how to prepare the food. We felt like we knew something that the people we had to serve would enjoy better than something like they were serving. Also they could be pretty hard to deal with. They demanded more money and they just didn't please us. So we got where we just did without the men that managed the cooking, and started training our colored boys who were washing the dishes. He would approach them and say, "How would you like to make twice as much money as you are making now?" "Yes sir, boss," they would say. And he would say, "Furthermore, if you do that as well as I want it, I wouldn't mind doubling it again."

So we trained four colored boys to do our cooking. Two worked at a time and they would really do what we wanted them to do. The people were happy with what they got because it was all supervised and we didn't fail to test it from time to time to see that it was right.

I think I made two or three cakes every morning and maybe a half dozen meringue pies and quite a few apple pies.

[The cooks] lived in the quarter of the black people, where they live now. We tried to treat them just like we'd like to be treated. They could have food to eat like we had and they served us well. No, I don't think there was [much for them to do otherwise in Myrtle Beach]. And this was something that a lot of people wouldn't have done. The policeman came to Mack and told him they had found that his cook had stolen mayonnaise (a case of gallons of Duke's mayonnaise) from our storeroom. It was not locked. So Mack said, "You do what you can about punishing him, but don't let him know that I know it." He said, "I don't want to do without him. I'll just watch him more closely." And so we kept him right on until we closed our business and sold it.

Leon was the main cook and Briscoe was another one. He did learn how to do a lot of the things that I formerly did, and we let him do them to make it easier for me.[67]

We retired and just started living like most socially inclined people would live, nothing extra, you know. Neither of us played cards or enjoyed it to the extent that some people do. So many people like to play cards and gamble. I think we did our gambling when we got here. [Laughter.]

And Julia's, too.

Epilogue

"See that lighter part of the clay?" A rectangular spot in the new-plowed field marks the dimensions of the old Pee Dee Baptist Academy, which was able to withstand decades better than flames. Next to the dirt, under a half-dozen interlocking live oaks—a composition of brick and bark—stands Wannamaker Church. Its plaque recites a succinct history: "Organized 1876. Burned July 1946. Rebuilt 1948." On this cool, bright morning in March, a hundred years after Gary Mincey was born in 1907, the author is trying to get a sense of what it was like for the first-grader to walk from his farmhouse to Wannamaker School.

"Could he have crossed this creek?" The questioning author gets out of the car, driven by Gary's son Carlisle (b. 1944), and traces the ditchwater as it disappears into the swamp amid brush, native cane and bare, skinny hardwoods. Swamps everywhere in this part of the county yield grudgingly to farmland, a reminder of the original terrain of Horry, yet the full-grown trees that once gave the area a venerable and even forbidding air are now an endangered species, protected from the saw mainly around houses and churches.

Carlisle and his daughter, Angel, who is visiting from out of state, have agreed to sponsor this tour. As the car drives down Pinckney Road, an arc of dirt runs off to the side of the pavement, a remnant of the old road. "That's where the Anderson house was," a farmstead marked by a small barn. "The dirt road used to be in front of that house there"—an abandoned structure with a now-rolling roof and blue doors. The old road crosses the new to make a space between a grove of trees, then crosses again to the other side as a path of grassy dirt. "There was a cattle dip there." "Right there used to be a house." Rows of brown dirt—each a deep V flanked by two wedges above it—become narrower toward the horizon; there, red maples bud against an indecisive sky of blue varied by swirls of cirrus and a patch of stratus. The tour continues. "That used to be a hog parlor" and "See, there was a creek right there." But the hydrology has changed too much, with the building of ditches, the ditching of creeks, and the gnawing of beavers, for the trio to get a sense of the boy's path.

Recovering the past is as hard as finding Gary's foot-logs. If you want to spot bear tracks on International Drive, you must search before the road becomes an entrance to Carolina Forest, a new city. If you want to visit Lloyd's Motel, you will behold a flashy beachwear-store (perhaps ironic, considering Lloyd's zeal for promoting the town). In an obsolete tobacco barn, if you dare to climb way up to a tier-pole, don't stand on it or Crack!

More feasible is recalling the past. These chapters attest to the vivacity of a once-isolated area—of the people who do the remembering, of their fellow citizens, and of their daily life: ferry-paddling, field-hollering, fish-salting, fish-trapping, seed-cleaning, excursion-taking, yawl-winching, bucket-riding, rider-weed-clearing, tobacco-bench-sleeping, cake-baking, raft-making, 'coon-hunting and Night-Watching.

Notes

DAVID CARR

1. See Dr. Compton's article, "Hearing Horry History," in the *IRQ* 27.1 (1993): 5. In a sad twist on the preservation of memories: when the author visited Dr. Compton in an assisted-living facility, he vividly recalled the interview with Carr, but later that day did not recall the author's request that he look over the transcription, or perhaps recall the author himself.

2. Dave's mother, Jane, was born in 1866 or '67; his father, Carolina, was born in 1863.

3. Baby Ray became a star of a book for children learning to read. He was so popular that *Child World Reader*, written by Sarah Withers (1873–1955), a graduate of Winthrop College and a national figure in education, changed its name to *The Baby Ray Book*. See <http://www.rootsweb.com/~scyork/LouisePettus/early.htm.> The author thanks Ms. Jamie Ligas and Ms. Allison Faix, reference librarians at CCU, as well as Ms. Gina Price White, Director of Archives and Special Collections, Louise Pettus Archives, Dacus Library, Winthrop University. The series that *The Reader* helped compose was first published in 1917, so David, a veteran, would have been over thirty years old when he learned his ABCs. But he speaks of himself as the same age as a schoolchild, so perhaps the book was in an earlier series.

4. Carr was born the year that the Wilmington, Chadbourn & Conway Line first reached Conway from Chadbourn, NC, and terminated at the

Waccamaw River. At about the turn of the century the Conway Coast and Western was laid out between the Waccamaw and the new village of Myrtle Beach. A drawbridge was constructed over the Waccamaw in 1904, about which time the railroad was extended from Conway to Aynor. Hoyt McMillan, "A Brief History of Railroads in Horry County, South Carolina," *IRQ* 2.1 (1968): 5–8.

5. Temporary, narrow-gauge railroad tracks were laid throughout the forest; logs were hauled by cart or dragged by cable to flatbed cars and lifted onto them. Such railways were also built by Mr. Carr's brother Albert (born in 1906 and interviewed by the author in 2003), who said that his brother was always good at "schemy" work, i.e., which required planning and engineering.

6. Carr recalls grisly details of combat. "That's when that man got shot down right 'side me. Sometime you gwine walking and you know how you hear about them spiers [snipers, whom he suggests by poking one finger through the fingers on his other hand] in trees, in the moss and they be in there hidin' with the rifle [aims imaginary gun]. And you come by and see o' your man fall—Well!—after a while another one. And you turn back and chase the way the ball went in him [points to his heart], when they get most of the tree [?] the old Frenchman holler "Camarade!" [Raises hands as if surrendering.] And take um [probably the bodies of German soldiers], the sword and chop your head off. And chop you in your belly and your guts come out. They be red. And you come back along there evening just as blue as—swell up on you. And them boys would cut their head off them and take them to the camp and cut the meat off and bile it and tek a candle and light it and put the skull away for a flambeau and that thing would show a light just like a lahmp. [Laughs once in a sort of cough.] But if they catch you doing things, they court martial you." [More stories follow, enhanced by dramatic gestures, then, lowering the volume of his voice, he reveals how he kept contraband liquor:] "Tie the bottle and put it between m' leg, and tie it around my waist. Then come and sarched me, no whiskey. They had a wooden toilet. I go there and take a nail and tack it underneath the end of the seat and ben' it and tek that string and tie it around that bottle and put it down in that toilet. [Laughs.] Where they couldn't find it."

7. This chemical weapon, an oily liquid, is an irritant that causes blisters on exposed skin. It was first used by Germany in 1917. According to Wikipedia, it was lethal in only 1 percent of cases but effective as an incapacitating agent—for example, "the eyes (if exposed) become sore and the eyelids swollen, possibly leading to conjunctivitis and blindness."

8. For the reception of black World War I veterans by white South Carolinians, see Walter Edgar, *South Carolina: A History* (Columbia: Univ. of South Carolina Press, 1998): 481.

9. Myrtle Beach farms was carved out of the swamp near the beginning of the twentieth century in order to plant vegetables for the loggers who worked for Burroughs & Collins.

FLORENCE "FLOSSIE" SARVIS MORRIS

10. This article, reprinted in the *Horry Herald*, Feb. 21, 1952, was again reprinted in the *IRQ* 2.2 (1968): 4. Neither item provided the exact date of the original publication.

11. Eddy Lake was a mill village and cove off Bull Creek, a connection between the Pee Dee and Waccamaw Rivers that forms the southern border of the county.

LILLIE LOUISE BROWN LATIMER & RUTH CLAY "SABE" WOODBURY

12. Remarkable testimony that blacks and whites attended class together, although separated, before the Segregation Highway was paved through the community.

13. Mary Beaty, 1824–1901, emigrated from Maine to work as a teacher for the children of Henry L. Buck, also from Maine. She married Thomas Beaty. Like Mrs. Woodbury's great-great grandmother, Mrs. Beaty had her children stolen away, at least figuratively. For her story, see Marjory Q. Langston, "Before and After 1870." *IRQ* 1.2 (1967): 13–14.

14. Through the early twentieth century, many people in Horry County tapped pine trees, especially the longleaf, for their gum, then distilled it into spirits of turpentine and rosin, a solid, translucent, amber-to-almost-black resin. Originally these substances, called naval stores, helped to waterproof wooden ships, but they came to have many industrial uses.

15. Female ancestors named by the half-sisters:
Mother: Sarah Brown (Clay)
Grandmother ("Gamma")—Martha Ann Brown
Great-grandmother—Sally Powell (sold)
Great-great grandmother—Unnamed.

16. The earthquake of August 31, 1886, originated near Charleston and killed more than a hundred people.

17. F.G. Burroughs (1834–1897), the county's most prominent businessman, had three sons, F.A. (b. 1872–1942), Donald (1891–1967), and Arthur (1881–1912). The reference is probably to a son, but if by chance "Mr. Burroughs" refers to two different people, Brown could have meant F.G.

18. See C. Lewis, *Horry County*, South Carolina, 184–86.

19. A copy of *The Autobiography of George A. Singleton* (Boston: Forum, 1964) is held in the South Caroliniana Library, Columbia, South Carolina. (For help in regard to this book the author thanks Paul Lewis of the USC-Aiken Library and Roberta Copp of the South Caroliniana Library.) During World War I, Singleton, like Dave Carr, went to France where he served briefly as a chaplain (pp. 89–123).

WOODROW W. LONG

20. For family names the author is indebted to Ruth L. Douthit, "Long Family Horry County, South Carolina." *IRQ* 20.3 (1986): 17–35. Woodrow omits the family's own civil war over land.

21. Dorethea adds that the house, still standing, was moved about two miles away to the St. Paul's area, where two descendants of slaves live.

22. This type has a wide, flat blade and a long handle. Dorethea notes that Bill Mack Long's broadaxe still exists, and that Grandfather Thompson was a blacksmith who made axes, hoes, etc.

23. The third interview ends with footage of Mr. Long as he stands near the live oak tree on Lakeland Drive that had once marked a corner of the Long plantation: its half-dozen trunk-size limbs ignore gravity to extend and divide into a massive green crown that bows and sways around waterfalls of Spanish moss.

LINK VEREEN

24. General Jim Vaught, who grew up knowing Link, had a different interpretation: the name "Donnie Grant" (he surmised) was a result of scrapes with the law in Columbia during the 1920s, and the earlobe was cut not by a windshield but a by a knife. A family story does include a window, however—one through which Link made a quick exit.

25. "My brother and I walked to the Waterway to ask for a job," wrote Woodrow Long in 1993. "The road was state highway but we did not meet a car nor did one pass on the twenty-eight miles that we walked [round-trip]. They were not hiring that day but my brother and friend later worked on the project." Document furnished by Dorethea Long.

26. His grandmother may have been referring to a rice plantation on the lower Waccamaw. As for the prison-like oversight, a relic of this practice was reported as late as 1899 by an anonymous passenger on a steamboat excursion from Conway to Georgetown. "Some say the negroes in Georgetown County, hardly know they are free. They are payed by the job, or task, the overseers have little platforms six or eight feet square, built on four posts with a shade over them to sit or lie in and watch the negroes work." "On the Waccamaw." *Horry Herald*, 15 June 1899: 2.

CARRIE DANIELS DOYLE

27. Carrying one passenger after another, along with an audiocassette recorder or notebook, Billy came away with this impression:
They had been as fair and generous as anyone could have been, given the fact they didn't want to go broke. Even though some reactions to the system were better than others, the persons I talked with almost always included the refrain: "Joseph Holliday and George Holliday never turned anyone away who was in need; and when it was all said and done, they had fed many a hungry family."

28. Holliday provides this valuable background for his interviews with Mrs. Doyle. "She was the daughter of Press Daniels, superintendent of the Baptist church in the early 1900s, the first president of the Galivants Ferry Democratic Club, and the first person to organize a stump speaking near the river in that little section of Galivants Ferry Township." (A biannual Democratic rally is still held on the grounds of the Pee Dee Farms headquarters.) Daniels worked as an overseer for three generations of Hollidays. Regarding Carrie herself:

> She was a seamstress living in Aynor in the 1960s when I first talked with her (and brought pants to hem). Standing 5 feet, 6 or 7 inches, she was bent over a little from her sewing as well as gardening, but with a sparkle in her eye and the loveliest, most graceful smile you can imagine, her frail arm fluttering toward me as I walked in, her fingers finally pressing my hand or arm, she was so happy for company.

Holliday explains that Carrie and Ed had lived in the red-shingled house a few yards west of the barn. "Ed worked in the store and also as a debt-collector during tobacco season, an occasion for drinking, Carrie said, for both himself and George Judson Holliday—on behalf of whom Ed 'cloaked it,' i.e., brought liquor hidden under a jacket or other garment.

Carrie recalled that Ed, who had been a store clerk and manager for George, would often fall asleep on the job, probably with the help of drink. From his back office GJH would tell someone in the spacious area up front (its gargantuan walk-in safe still stands): 'Go out there and wake up the president.'" Billy remembers that after Carrie retold another of George's sardonic wisecracks, she "smiled and chuckled, her hand fluttering up to cover either a cheek full of snuff or the absence of teeth, I don't recall which."

29. Here is a technical description of Mrs. Doyle's variety of speech. It is the work of Prof. Stephen J. Nagle of Coastal Carolina University, co-editor with Sara L. Sanders of *English in the Southern United States* (Cambridge and New York: Cambridge Univ. Press, 2003). He lists four distinguishing features. **A.** Related to other Scots-Irish influenced dialects of the Southeast, mostly piedmont or mountains: e.g., (1) "a-prefixing" on present participles (archaically retained from Old English: *a-rarin'*, *a-quarrelin'*, *a-fishin'*, *a-settin'*; (2) pronominal *hit*, alternating with *it*, mostly for sentential/topical focus; certain regularized preterits such as *knowed*, common also in Appalachia, which has strong Scots-Irish roots. (But *knowed* is found in other vernaculars as well.) **B.** Related to African-American vernaculars: e.g., (1) *de* (d + schwa, that is, pronounced 'duh' not 'dee'; (2) *tote*, often viewed as a Bantu word, though there are some folks who argue for an Indo-European origin. **C.** All but unique to the coastal areas from outlying Virginia to the Lumbee community and obviously here as well: *was/weren't* regularization. *Was* becomes the default affirmative ("All them mules was named"), singular or plural; weren't becomes the default negative ("there weren't much tobacca"), singular or plural. This is not generally found in any other area of the South, to my knowledge. **D.** An innovative, evolving trans-Southern form: the vowel sound in *theecket*, identified by Labov as part of what he calls the Southern Shift, a change in progress. There are plenty of other vernacular features, of course, especially the leveling of various irregular forms of the preterit and past participle ("He run that old blacksmith shop"); demonstrative *them* ("them mules") for *those*.

30. Francis was the half-brother of Billy's grandfather George. George was the son of Joseph William Holliday, who first married Mary Elizabeth Grissette (mother of George) and then her sister Nettie (mother of Francis).

31. Preston M. Coleman (c. 1878–1954), was overseer for George J. Holliday, disabled in his last days. Carrie was hired as a nursemaid for his son, Stanley D. (b. 1915), whose own interview conducted in 1993 provides many details about the Holliday clan and Galivants Ferry.

32. Billy Holliday sheds light on this arrangement. "The various agricultural enterprises that the Ferry community supported stemmed ultimately from the economic system that the South was left with in the 1870s on into the 1930s. Historians refer to it as 'time-supply mercantilism.' It was the only way people back then could get credit for food and clothes and even for farm implements and fertilizer. It was a harsh system involving crop liens and land mortgages. The borrowers thus paid interest not only on the loan but virtually on their purchases as well, due to markups. The merchants realized that they themselves and the successful, borrowing farmers would virtually be subsidizing the failures. Very few farmers really understood what was going on financially." See also Edgar T. Thompson, "Country Store." *Encyclopedia of Southern Culture*, ed. Charles Reagan Wilson and William Ferris (Chapel Hill: Univ. of NC Press, 1989): 15–18.

33. As Stanley D. Coleman, a neighbor of Catherine Lewis, remembered it: "Mama didn't want me to play with the black ones and they were the only ones that would do everything I wanted them to do. There were a number of black ones on the Ferry but not near as many as whites, and as far as I know, nobody tried to mix them." He points out that the Deadline, which marked where Negroes were not allowed to spend the night, ended not far down the Pee Dee Highway at Jordanville (Interview 13 Oct. 1993: 17).

34. "The 'Keeley Cure' was a treatment for alcoholism developed by a Dr. Keeley in the nineteenth century. He established sanitariums in many cities around the nation. The Keeley Cure involved a treatment of several weeks of group therapy and some medicinal bromides rumored to contain minute amounts of gold. The Cure had a good success rate." Professor Eldred E. "Wink" Prince, Coastal Carolina University. Carrie may be referring specifically to the Keeley Institute, a clinic for alcoholics that was housed in Rome, Georgia, in the early 1900s. See Digital Library of Georgia.

35. The barge-polers, especially Will Marlowe, announced their arrival by blowing a curved horn—J.W.F.H. Carrie was born the year Mary B. Beaty, the woman for whom Thomas Brown ran a distillery, died.

36. In the Great Depression, these began as Fords pulled by mules, then developed into flat-bed carts made from the front axle and wheels of a vehicle and pulled by an animal.

37. Walter Hill, Curator of History at the Horry County Museum, writes: "I am assuming she meant a regular kerosene lamp but without the glass. I imagine after the chimney or glass was broken it was expensive to replace and perhaps it was cheaper to purchase one without the glass. If lit without

the glass chimney, it will just flicker and smoke, but the chimney draws better causing the flame to rise and burn cleaner and brighter as well as prevent wind from blowing it out."

38. Long since razed, it had originally been the little commissary in the early 1800s called Evans Store. In 1869 JWH took it and the surrounding land over—JWFH.

RILLA COOK MCCRACKIN

39. These companies also sold other products. "In the early 1900s many salesmen went from door-to-door selling spices; Golden Rule, Watkins, Raleigh, and McNess were some of the well-known brands." Ann A. Hertzler, "Herbs and Spices." Virginia Cooperative Extension. Publication 348-907. July 1997. <www.ext.vt.edu/pubs/foods/348-907/348-907.html>

40. The squirrel botfly is parasitic in its larval stage. As it grows under the skin, it makes a lump called a "warble," probably the origin of the mistaken term "wolf." Prof. James O. Luken, Coastal Carolina Univ., e-mail to the author, 2006.

GARY M. MINCEY & DOUGLAS B. BAILEY

41. Nickname for what was actually a law against not having fences. It required people to impound their cows and pigs. Before this law, cattle would even make their way to the beach where they stood waiting for a sea breeze to cool them and blow away insects. See interview with Andrew Stanley, April 1991. Also Lucille Burroughs Godfrey, "Excerpts from the Burroughs Family." *IRQ* 4.3 (1970): 7.

42. For the confessions of a former and impenitent law-breaker, see Ann Long's interview with Marion Moore of Bucksport and Sandy Island (1993). Mincey was renowned as a fisherman: "He said that since God created the world three-fourths water," writes his granddaughter, "He meant for men to fish three-fourths of the time, so he did." She adds that Gary knew every river, lake, slough and landing in the state.

43. See P.L. Elvington, "Brief History of Pee Dee Baptist Academy." *IRQ* 11.3 (1977): 30. Also C. Lewis, "Pee Dee Baptist Academy." *IRQ* 24.4 (1990): 31-32. To Catherine, this venture was a precursor to the community's effort to found Coastal Carolina College in 1954.

44. This is a vaguely defined area near the Lumber River, and its schoolhouse, once located next to the railroad tracks between Fair Bluff and Nichols, is no more visible in the swamp than Doug's raccoon.

45. Doug's father was Rufus Albert Bailey (1882–1956), and his mother, Della Hill Bailey, died when he was two years old. Rufus remarried Lona Charity Arnette (1887–1963). This information was supplied by Singleton Bailey, Doug's son.

46. Gary, who lived until 2001, was remembered by his granddaughter as a man who, except on Sunday, smelled of pipe tobacco and fish. "He wore 'old men' hats, told great stories and could quote the Bible thoroughly. There were few people who didn't know him or hadn't heard of him. I have never heard anyone say anything bad about him. Their comments usually pertained to his humor, fairness and knowledge. He was respected." Lynda Todd, a colleague of Doug Bailey, remembers Doug as kind and caring. "Nothing made him happier than to help someone. He had a way of communicating with the customers that put them at ease. People that did not go to the doctor would come to him for his opinion, and he would always help them. Everyone called him 'Dr. Bailey.'" (Personal correspondence with the author, 2007.) Lewis Gould, b. 1913, was a leader in the black community of Loris and the stock manager at Loris Drug Store. Interviewed by Catherine Lewis in 1990, he reported starting his career there in 1950. At the beginning, for three months of the year, he worked as a cook at camp run by Future Farmers of America. "What do they pay you down there?" asked Doug Bailey. Hearing the answer, he said, "I'll pay you that year around. Come back here and stay." Gould adds: "I tell people you couldn't find—there might be some just as good but there ain't none better than he is nowhere."

S.F. HORTON

47. See Peter A. Coclanis, "David R. Coker, Pedigreed Seeds and Limits of Agribusinesses in Early Twentieth-Century South Carolina." *Business & Economic Theory* 28.2 (Fall 1999): 105–14.

48. Crotalaria is a genus of herbaceous plants and woody shrubs popularly known as "rattlepods." Prof. Prince notes that because it produces high levels of nitrogen, farmers planted it as a soil-builder— i.e., a soil-enricher. Prince is the author, with Robert R. Simpson, of *Long Green: The Rise and Fall of Tobacco in South Carolina* (Athens Univ. of Georgia Press, 2000).

49. A foundation seed is what the grower uses to raise certified seed. Its origins are defined and its growth monitored for off-types, cleanliness and uniformity. (Bruce Johnson, Horry County Extension Agent with Clemson University, 2006.)

50. In 2006 Jeanne Morgan Turner told a story about Mr. Horton that took place a year or so after the death of his wife Rebecca. "One afternoon after dining at one of Loris' fine eating establishments my husband and I were paying our bill and Mr. S.F. was behind us. He told me to get in his car because he had something he wanted to show me. I told him my husband would have to go and he said he would have to sit in the back seat. Being a little apprehensive—he was over ninety-two and had the reputation of driving over the speed limit—we climbed in his large Chevy Caprice Classic and set out for an adventure. Down the Daisy Highway we rode and then turned onto a narrow dirt road that led to a vast area of fields of corn, tobacco, soybeans, etc., in full growth. We would stop at one field and then the next and he would tell us how he had developed a specific fertilizer for this crop and that crop, even showing us the drainage ditches he had constructed for his tobacco fields. How proud he was of the crops that were 'coming in' even if he only leased out the land. After almost an hour we were delivered back to the restaurant to retrieve our vehicle. Mr. S.F. is in my dad's Sunday school class and I've always asked how he was doing each Sunday. I guess he just took a likin' to me because of my daddy."

ANDREW STANLEY

51. Jackie Stanley explains that mutton corn was broken right off the stalk and cooked green before it got hard enough to grind into grits or meal.
52. Ms. Stanley explains that many people often cooked outside. They built a fire in a pit and placed tin wire over it to support the food or vessels. They also placed wash pots on the hot ashes to "boil" the white clothes clean on washday, or to cook corn, peanuts and potatoes just as in a chimney. Indoors, chimneys were also used to cook food; potatoes and peanuts were cooked and roasted underneath the ashes, or "boil-pots" pots were placed in the chimneys for cooking beans, meat or whatever.
53. If Link was fifteen years older than Andrew, he would have been born in 1888 or 1889 and would have been about thirty years old when he took the fifteen-year-old mail carrier across the river around 1918. But Donnie says he himself was only fifteen or sixteen when he operated the ferry. Perhaps he held that job at two phases or his life, or on and off for at least fifteen years. Another mystery.
54. In the 1860 Census of Horry County, a James Bessent, age twenty-one, is listed as a child of W.A. Bessent (family 973). Compiled by Ione Woodall. *IRQ* 21.2 (1987).

55. For more details about such treatment, see the interview with Mr. Henry Small of Burgess-Freewoods, which was conducted by Catherine Lewis and the author.

JULIA PRYOR MACKLEN

56. Mr. Macklen purchased this motel from the Elliots. "It was actually his third motel, the first being pretty small and located near Spivey's [Beach] south of Myrtle Beach downtown. It was probably sold when he purchased Travelers Motel"—RPM.

57. "Somehow," writes Robert, "he was convinced by Clarence to buy the grocery store and quit his job in Pennsylvania. He sold the home, furniture, etc., all without a word with Mother about such a change."

58. The Patricia Inn (same as the Manor) was built in 1941 at Twenty-eighth Ave. on Ocean Blvd. and was razed in 1985. See J. Marcus Smith, "Patricia's end," *Sun News* (Myrtle Beach, SC): 7 Sept. 2000.

59. Later she tells more details about the hardscrabble grocery business. "There were so few people here and we were having so little business, that the need was urgent that we sell something. So we would serve the people if they came to the store, but if they didn't come, there were times when my husband would go to them and ask if they wouldn't like something he had particularly good that day. Then he'd come back to the store and fill the order, go back and deliver it to them, wait a week, and then collect from them. We were the first people in Myrtle Beach who required a customer to sign a ticket when they charged something. And we had people—one lady in particular whose husband was the only barber here. She would spend I don't know how long looking at her tickets, trying her best to convince us that that one was not signed by her." [Laughter.]

60. "All five children loved Jessie"—RPM.

61. Towering over the beach at Fifty-fifth St. N, the "Million Dollar Hotel" was finished in 1929 and razed in 1974, having gone from the frying pan of Depression to the fire of obsolescence.

62. "As important a place as the Patricia Manor was," Mrs. Macklen says later in the interview, "the lady used to drive the truck—it was a Ford—and come down to select her produce and food, mainly seafood at that time, and then take it to Patricia Manor. People who had the money to own a business like that wouldn't think of doing that today."

63. The motel bordered a horseshoe-shaped driveway that enclosed a grassy area—RPM.

64. The earlier motel was Ocean Pines. "The Macklens' last home of any sort was Travelers Motor Hotel. We all lived in more of a house environment. Even the office for registration of guests was our living room and we had a kitchen, dining room, bedrooms all under one roof like 'home.' At Lloyd's [their next motel] Mother & Dad had a bedroom that was connected to the office to rent rooms. The doorbell rang as late as midnight. The children slept in various rooms of the motel, so it was hard for parents to keep up with where we were. Mother never had a real home till they lived in the house where you met her." RPM.

65. "Mother had to be a Queen to live with the King"—RPM. Another person declared that she worked like a slave; but in any case, hard work did not kill her, for she lived until 2001.

66. Kings Highway became U.S. 17, which had until then been routed through Marion and Florence. "Dad did have lots to do with the development of a new Hwy. 17, so Myrtle Beach got more traffic and the Ocean Highway Association was formed." When the Macklens lived in Travelers Motel, "Kings Highway was a two-lane concrete road which had a one-lane dirt road parallel to the pavement." They paved this dirt road and added it to the highway in the early 1940s. "The bridge was built across Chesapeake Bay near Norfolk, VA; before that north and south traffic could require a two-to-three-hour delay to cross the bay with a ferry. This gave tourists good cause to travel on Hwy. 301 via Florence, SC"—RPM.

67. "'H.B.' Hemingway and Leon Livingston worked as cooks for Lloyd's almost to the end. The waitress folks always applied pressure to these cooks: 'Where's my steak and seafood orders?' Naturally the cooks were going as fast as they could and did not choose to be sassy or talk back. So they said just one word loud and clear, 'Working.' This was smart of them. Never heard a fuss because of it. I would love to see these men again. They were all about my age and I think I learned a lot of mutual feelings and respect. I suppose Mother and Dad knew more blacks than anyone"—RPM, who began working with African Americans in 1935.

Please visit us at
www.historypress.net